NAVIGATING

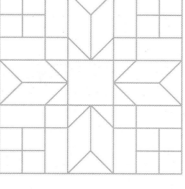

COMPASS

DESIGNS

BARBARA ANN CARON

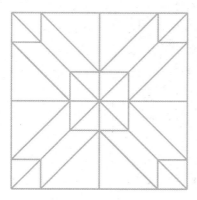

American Quilter's Society

P. O. Box 3290 • Paducah, KY 42002-3290

Located in Paducah, Kentucky, the American Quilter's Society (AQS), is dedicated to promoting the accomplishments of today's quilters. Through its publications and events, AQS strives to honor today's quiltmakers and their work — and inspire future creativity and innovation in quiltmaking.

EDITOR: BONNIE BROWNING
COPY EDITOR: BARBARA SMITH
BOOK DESIGN/ILLUSTRATIONS: LANETTE BALLARD & WHITNEY HOPKINS
COVER DESIGN: ELAINE WILSON
PHOTOGRAPHY: CHARLES R. LYNCH, UNLESS INDICATED OTHERWISE

Library of Congress Cataloging-in-Publication Data

Caron, Barbara Ann
     Navigating compass designs / Barbara Ann Caron.
               p.   cm.
     Includes bibliographical references (p. 158-159).
     ISBN 0-89145-896-4
     1. Patchwork--Patterns. 2. Patchwork quilts. 3. Compass in art.
4. Circle in art.   I. Title
TT835.C37414   1998
746.46'041--dc21   98-27957
                                                  CIP

Additional copies of this book may be ordered from: American Quilter's Society, PO Box 3290, Paducah, KY 42002-3290 @ $19.95. Add $2.00 for postage & handling.

Printed in the U.S.A. by Image Graphics, Paducah, KY

CONTENTS

INTRODUCTION 4

■ **CHAPTER 1:**

Concept and Context 5

■ **CHAPTER 2:**

Drafting Basics 12

■ **CHAPTER 3:**

Planning and Execution 21

■ **CHAPTER 4:**

Designs 36

Design 1:
　　Mariner's Compass, Palm Leaf,
　　Elongated Dogtooth Border 37
Design 2:
　　Mariner's Compass, Baltimore Belle,
　　Split Squares Border 42
Design 3:
　　Mariner's Compass, Star and Cross,
　　Squares on Point Border 47
Design 4:
　　Slashed Star, Best of All,
　　Shaded Sawtooth Border .52
Design 5:
　　Sunburst, Blackford's Beauty,
　　Sunbeams Border 57
Design 6:
　　Chips and Whetstones, Amish Star,
　　Dogtooth and Split Squares Border 62
Design 7:
　　Arabian Star, Wood Lily,
　　Dogtooth and Squares Border 67

Design 8:
　　Kansas Sunflower, Old Maid's Ramble,
　　Diamonds Border 72
Design 9:
　　Sunflower, Kansas Troubles,
　　Sawtooth Border 77
Design 10:
　　Marigold, Auntie's Favorite©,
　　Checkerboard Border 82
Design 11:
　　Sunflower, Country Roads,
　　Triangles Border 87
Design 12:
　　Single Sunflower, Wyoming Valley,
　　Dogtooth Border 92
Design 13:
　　Wheel of Fortune, Joseph's Coat,
　　Broken Dishes Border 97
Design 14:
　　Feathered Star, Shaded Crossroad©
　　Surrounded Squares Border 102
Design 15:
　　Rising Sun, Wild Goose Chase,
　　Birds in Flight Border 107
Design 16:
　　Sunbirds, Odd Fellows,
　　Flying Geese Border 112

■ **CHAPTER 5:**

Variations .117

Appendices

A. Circular Grids 123

B. Quilt Layouts to Color 126

C. Six-inch Blocks 142

Bibliography 158

About the Author 159

INTRODUCTION

Like many quiltmakers, I have always appreciated the striking visual impact of circular patchwork designs. In 1986, I began to share my enthusiasm for these designs through a workshop, Patchwork in a Circle. This book evolved from my interest and teaching experiences. Although the concept of alternate setting blocks is added, fourteen of the circular patchwork designs are taken from my original workshop handout. I hope you enjoy working with these designs as much as I do.

Design 1: Mariner's Compass, Palm Leaf, and Elongated Dogtooth Border.
By the author, 1997.

Concept and Context

For centuries, circular patchwork designs have been appreciated for their exquisite beauty. They are thought appropriate for masterpiece quilts because they are considered technically difficult to piece. Unfortunately, this belief has tended to intimidate all but the most experienced quiltmaker, and that need not be the case.

This book makes circular patchwork designs, including compasses, sunflowers, and other more unusual designs, accessible to a broad audience. It addresses design sources, pattern drafting, and all aspects of planning and executing a quilt.

The Concept

Traditionally, most quilts based on circular patchwork designs use block-to-block or sashed settings. While some of these quilts are quite lovely, others are less interesting. Some nineteenth century quilts incorporate appliqué motifs with the circular designs, and the effect is quite beautiful. However, the inspiration for this book is a design in *Keepsake Quilts*, a booklet edited by Mabel Obenchain for Famous Features, a syndicated mail-order source that began selling patterns in the 1940s. The booklet's red and white cover quilt, pieced by Betty Harriman of Bruceton, Missouri, combines 17" Kansas Sunflower and Kansas Troubles blocks. A sawtooth border completes the quilt. A modified version of Harriman's quilt is included as Design 9 in this book.

Recognizing that an alternate setting block can add a dynamic visual quality when used in combination with the more static circular design, I began to collect interesting circular and setting-block patterns. Both classic and less well-known circular designs were selected, and setting blocks were chosen for their strong diagonal movement. Combining two types of blocks in a quilt not only created an exciting visual impact, but also significantly reduced the total number of circular blocks that must be pieced. To enhance the body of the quilt, pieced borders were also included.

The original plan for this book was to design 12 quilts, but that number ultimately grew to 16. There were so many beautiful blocks from which to choose. To facilitate construction, in several cases, the designs were modified or simplified. All the compasses used here have 16 rather than 32 or 64 points. Modifications have been made to some of the setting blocks, too. Design changes are noted in the text that accompanies each pattern. As for construction techniques, a combination of piecing and appliqué was often used to assemble circular patchwork designs. However, for more accuracy, this book recommends using only piecing. You may, however, prefer to appliqué the smallest of the center circles in the miniature blocks.

As the book developed, it became clear that

many different combinations of circular and setting blocks and borders can work well together. The blocks and borders may be used interchangeably. In fact, the patterns can be used to make more than 4,000 different quilts by using the blocks and borders in different combinations. Each design is provided in two sizes: a 12" block and a 6" miniature block. With the blocks in these two sizes, quiltmakers have even more beautiful possibilities from which to choose.

THE CONTEXT

The designs represented are organized according to pictorial quality and structure. The three categories based on pictorial quality are compass/star, sunflower/sun, and miscellaneous. These groupings are not entirely separate. Over the years, the same basic design is often identified by a variety of names. For example, Designs 3, 4, and 5 are commonly identified today as Mariner's Compasses. Yet, historically these designs include both star and sun references. Generally compass/star designs have triangular or kite-shaped points that project outward from a small center, usually a circle. The sunflower/sun designs have diamond-shaped petals or small triangles that project from a large center circle. The first seven designs in this book are considered compasses or stars, the next five are considered sunflowers or suns, and the final four designs fall into the miscellaneous category. The designs in the miscellaneous category are, for the most part, less commonly found in existing quilts and published patterns.

The three structural categories refer to the number of points or divisions found in the design. Historically, the largest number of circular patchwork designs are based on multiples of four points/divisions. The first 10 designs in this book fit into that category and have 8 or 16 points. Less common are designs based on multiples of five, such as the sunflower in Design 11. The remaining designs are based on multiples of six and have 12 or 24 points. Not included in this book are circular patchwork designs with a structure based on multiples of nine. Such designs are relatively rare, but can be found in existing quilts and published patterns. Also found in some quilts are designs with an apparently arbitrary number of points/divisions, such as 17 or 29. One can only assume the quiltmaker was appliquéing rather than piecing a design and continued to add points, without regard for number, until she had a circle. It is intriguing to think about when, where, and how quiltmakers got their designs and what form the designs took, especially before the 1890s when published patterns for the most common designs became available.

QUILT DESIGNS AND SOURCES

According to quilt scholar Barbara Brackman, the earliest date-inscribed Mariner's Compass is found in a 1726 English quilt, while the earliest date-inscribed American quilt is from 1834. The compass design can be found in quilts that are thought to be earlier, but they are not date-inscribed, such as a scrap quilt (c. 1800) in the Baltimore County Historical Society. This quilt has 16 full and 14 half-compasses that are based on a 24-point design. The quilt has a diagonal block-to-block setting that is interrupted by a central sunburst motif constructed solely of 45° diamonds.

While some early nineteenth century compass quilts can be found, this design appears to have become widely popular in America by the middle of century. Among surviving quilts, there are 20-, 24-, 32-, 40-, 48-, and 64-point versions of compass designs.

An outstanding quilt in the Newark (New Jersey) Museum was made by Catherine A. Fitzgerald of Newark (c. 1840). Catherine won three state prizes for her striking red and cream Princess Feather and Rising Sun quilt. The 20 pieced compasses in this quilt have 32 points. The compasses alternate with large appliquéd Princess Feathers.

The Newark Museum
Art Resource, NY

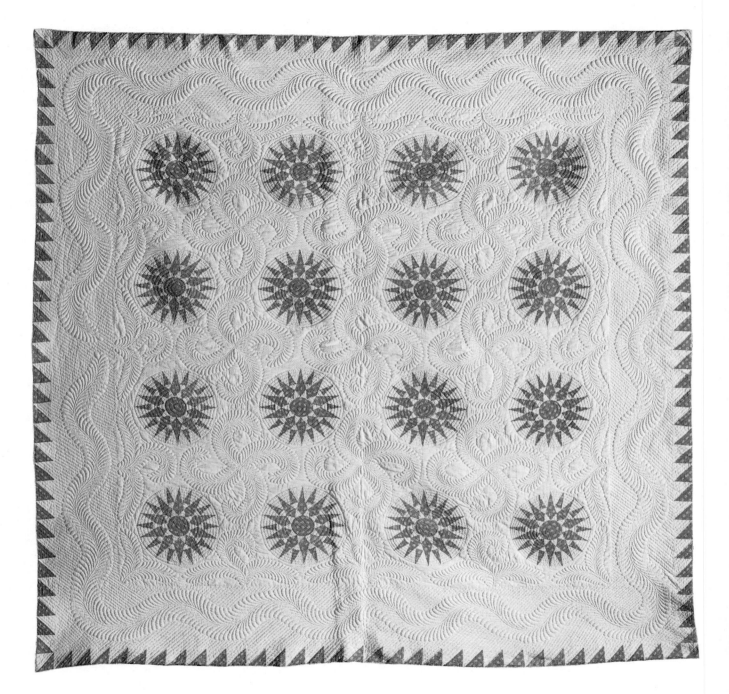

Also from the mid-nineteenth century is a 20-point compass design by Anna Sophie Shriver of Funkstown, Maryland. Now housed in The National Museum of American History (Smithsonian Institution), this red and white quilt has an elaborate quilting design consisting of Princess Feathers between the 20 compasses, and a serpentine feather between the body of the quilt and the sawtooth outermost border.

Smithsonian Institution

Another exceptional nineteenth century quilt, made by Emeline Barker of New York City, bears a close resemblance to the Mariner's Compass and Hickory Leaf quilt described on page 10. Barker's quilt is similar in its overall size as well as its use of nine 64-point compasses and small appliquéd abstract floral motifs between the pieced blocks. However, Barker's quilt is executed in blue, red, and olive green on a white background and has a pieced border of triangles.

Emeline Barker quilt, 44.310,
Museum of City of New York

The Shelburne Museum in Shelburne, Vermont, owns a magnificent Mariner's Compass and Hickory Leaf quilt that dates to the 1830s or 1840s. The nine large (approximately 30") compasses, in navy, yellow, and white or navy, red, and white, have 64 very narrow points. Navy and red hickory-leaf and orange slice motifs fill the spaces between the compasses, and a printed border fabric completes the quilt. While the quilt-maker is unknown, this quilt is thought to have a New Jersey origin.

Not all compass designs were so elaborate or contained so many points. For example, the Shelburne Museum's collection also includes a red, white, and blue Mariner's Compass (c. 1850) by Mary Canfield Benedict Baker that has only 16 points.

According to Carrie Hall in *The Romance of the Patchwork Quilt*, the Sunflower design originated in Connecticut around 1825. Certainly by the mid-nineteenth century, the design was popular with quiltmakers from Canada to Texas and from the East Coast to the Midwest, as evidenced by the many existing quilts that exhibit this design.

One attractive example of the sunflower design is a quilt (c. 1840–1880) in the Philadelphia Museum of Art. Identified by the name Heart and Compass, it contains thirty 18-point sunflower blocks that have appliquéd hearts at the corners and a stylized appliquéd border of flowers and birds. A New Jersey signature quilt (c. 1850) combines 16-point sunflowers with a sashing of appliquéd oak leaves, an inner border of pieced and appliquéd flowers, and a sawtooth border. A scrap sunflower quilt (c. 1850) in Seattle's Museum of History and Industry has a diagonal setting that is unusual and visually complex because the quilt's 12-point sunflower block design incorporates 4-patch blocks at the corners. When set block-to-block, this setting results in the appearance of multiple strips of sashing.

While there are many early examples of compass/star and sunflower/sun quilt designs, there are fewer examples of the other types of designs included in this book.

Historically, there is an obvious visual relationship between compasses that appeared on sea charts and compass designs that appeared in early quilts. While compass quilts have been documented along the East Coast, by the middle of the nineteenth century, the design was found in several other parts of the country, including Kentucky, Ohio, Indiana, and Texas. Later in the century, there are examples from other states, too. However, it should also be recognized that compasses are related to basic geometric, starlike motifs that have been used in the decorative arts of many cultures for thousands of years, and certainly before about 1395 when cartographers began to decorate maps with compasses. Circular geometric shapes that represent the stars, sun, and moon, as well as flowers, can be found in the ruins of ancient civilizations and in the artifacts of more recent cultures. These shapes are visually effective and yet easy to draw with simple instruments.

There are many examples of the use of decorative circular designs similar to those found in quilts during the last two centuries. The hex signs that began to appear in Europe during the Middle Ages are basic circular designs. Compass-like stars are found in Arabic designs, including twelfth- and fourteenth-century wall and floor mosaics, as well as thirteenth- and fourteenth-century woven fabrics. In 1525, Albrecht Durer published instructions on compass-constructed geometric forms that were intended for use by artisans working in a variety of media. This type of ornament was especially popular in northern Europe, where its applications included chip carving. By the eighteenth century in America, the Pennsylvania Dutch used the same basic design principles for hex signs that decorated their furniture. These signs were used on their barns in the nineteenth century. Nineteenth-century furniture pattern books provided directions for decorative star shapes. Abstract star or floral motifs appeared in Victorian architecture by the mid-nineteenth century.

Circular designs are not only visually appealing but also relatively commonplace in the decorative arts. Their use in early quilts, therefore, should come as no surprise. Continued use and wide distribution of these designs were probably facilitated by the availability of printed quilt patterns. The Ladies Art Company included a number of circular patchwork designs in its catalogs, beginning in the 1890s. These designs were also published and widely distributed by mail-order pattern services and in books. Today, some of these same circular patchwork designs continue to appeal to quiltmakers.

#9 Kansas Trouble
#15 Rising Sun
#7 Dogtooth and Square Border

DRAFTING BASICS

While 12" and 6" blocks and corresponding borders are provided for all the designs in this book, a knowledge of pattern drafting gives quiltmakers the ability to produce blocks and quilts of any size. It also fosters creativity, because it provides the quiltmaker with the knowledge necessary to modify traditional designs or to create original designs.

The easiest way to draft any patchwork design is to use an underlying grid that corresponds to the basic geometric structure of the design. Creating that grid is the most difficult step in drafting circular patchwork designs. The grid contains radiating lines that divide a circle at intervals appropriate to the particular design. The number and location of the lines is determined by the design, with most designs based on multiples of four, five, or six. For example, drafting a design with 32 divisions uses lines located at 11¼° intervals. That is, a 360° circle divided by 32 points is marked at intervals of 11¼°. For a design requiring 40 divisions, the interval is 9°, and for a design requiring 48 divisions, the interval is 7½°. To locate these intervals, use polar coordinate graph paper, marked in one-degree increments. This paper is available in office- and drafting-supply stores.

While polar coordinate graph paper is much easier to use than a protractor, it is still difficult to accurately mark increments of less than a full degree. For this kind of accuracy use computer designing and drafting programs to make the lines. A computer was used to create the three circular grids found on pages 123 – 125. Using these grids, quiltmakers can accurately draft patterns based on multiples of four, five, or six, so designs that require 8, 10, 12, 16, 20, 24, 32, 40, or 48 divisions can be drafted using the appropriate grid.

THE GRID METHOD: A STEP-BY-STEP DRAFTING EXERCISE

Assemble basic supplies and tools, including paper, tape, ruler or straight edge, pencils, compass, and circular grids.

GETTING STARTED

Choose a circular patchwork design and count the points to determine whether it is based on multiples of 4, 5, or 6 divisions. Then select the appropriate circular grid (pages 123 – 125). If the design has 8, 16, or 32 divisions, use the grid for multiples of four. If it has 10, 20, or 40 divisions, use the grid for multiples of five. Designs with 12, 24, or 48 divisions require the grid for multiples of six. Information on the number of divisions required to draft the designs in this book is provided in Chapter 4. For other designs, simply count the number of points and determine whether they are evenly divisible by four, five, or six. Most designs require the same number of drafting divisions as points, but a few need twice as many drafting divisions as points.

The Slashed Star from Design 4 is used for this step-by-step exercise. It has 16 points and uses the grid for multiples of four.

On a large piece of paper, draw a square representing the desired finished block size. It is easier to draw an accurate square if graph paper is used, even though graph paper squares are not needed for drafting circular designs. Locate and mark the center of the square and draw a + that divides the paper square vertically and horizontally. Lay the grid on top of the paper, matching the center marks and making certain that the edges of the paper and the grid line up on all four sides. Drafting tape is ideal for attaching the grid to the paper because it comes off easily without damaging the paper (Figure 2–1).

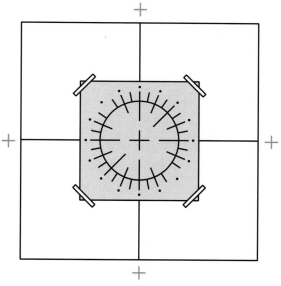

Figure 2–1

DRAWING THE OUTER CIRCLE

Using a compass anchored precisely at the center of the paper and grid, draw a circle the desired radius (Figure 2–2). In this book, the large circular designs have a radius of 5" and the small designs have a radius of 2½". Make certain the lead is sharp so the line is crisp. Compasses are widely available at office and drafting supply stores. While it is not necessary to purchase an expensive compass, choose a brand that is well-made and holds its position securely, so the radius does not shift as the circle is drawn. Compasses designed for architectural and mechanical drafting have locking screws that help maintain a consistent radius.

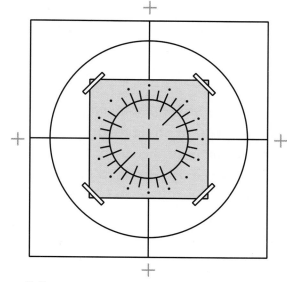

Figure 2–2

Compasses come in a variety of sizes. Most small compasses can draw a radius of up to 5 inches. Larger compasses and compass extensions are also available. To draw very large circles, use a yardstick beam compass. It consists of a lead holder and separate point, each with a slot that holds a standard wooden yardstick. With this tool, it is possible to draft circular designs with radii of nearly three feet. Some plastic quilting rulers have small holes at half-inch intervals that can be used in combination with a push pin and sharp pencil to draw circles, but only at intervals determined by the ruler. Using a string with a push pin at one end and a pencil at the other is not recommended because the string may stretch and vary the measurements. Since a satisfactory compass can be purchased for less than five dollars, it is a better choice and a worthwhile investment.

Notice that here, and throughout the book, the circular patchwork designs are smaller than the background squares. That is, the 12-inch squares have 10-inch circular designs and the 6-inch squares have 5-inch circular designs. The advantage of smaller circles in larger background squares is the flexibility to trim the background squares slightly, if necessary, so they are the same size as the pieced setting squares. Another advantage of the smaller circles is that they are more easily pieced into background squares.

TRANSFERRING THE GRID MARKINGS

Select a ruler or straight edge that is longer than the diameter of the circle. The diameter is two times the radius, so a block that has a 5-inch radius has a 10-inch diameter. Make certain the ruler has no nicks that might create a crooked line. Lay the ruler over the paper and grid and connect pairs of marks that are directly opposite each other on the grid circle. Make certain the ruler passes through the center point of the grid (Figure 2–3).

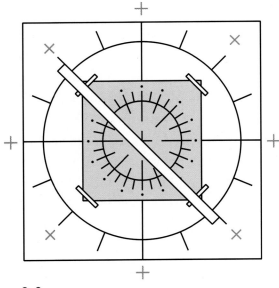

Figure 2–3

Using a sharp pencil, draw short marks that touch the outer circle drawn in the previous step.

Draw only the number of marks required for the design. In this example, only the 16 grid lines with dots are needed. To facilitate the drafting process, it is helpful to use one color to mark the eight major lines. These are the longest lines (+ and x) on the grid in Figure 2–3, shown in tan. Use another color to mark the intermediate lines, the gray mid-length lines on the grid. (If the other 16 short grid lines are needed to draw a design, mark them in some other color.)

ADDING CIRCLES AND CONNECTING MARKS

Remove the circular grid since it is no longer needed. Using a compass anchored precisely at the center of the paper, draw the additional circle(s) required by the design. The radius of each circle is provided. The Slashed Star, in this example, requires a 1½" radius inner circle. Next, connect the opposite pairs of dashes with a light line (Figure 2–4). All these lines should pass through the center of the paper. However, unless the design actually divides the center circle, the lines can stop where they intersect that circle. All the lines required to draft the compass/star or sunflower/sun design are drawn by connecting marks on one circle to marks on the other circle(s).

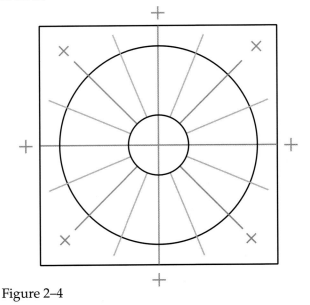

Figure 2–4

DRAFTING THE MAJOR POINTS

Using the original drawing of the design as a reference, draw the eight large points. Connect the marks on the outer circle to the appropriate marks on the inner circle (Figure 2–5). Only the tan + and x grid lines are required for this step. It is usually easier to start with the vertical and horizontal (+) points and then add the diagonals (x). After the eight large points have been drawn, notice that eight small triangles surround the center circle. They are created by the overlapping legs of the large star points.

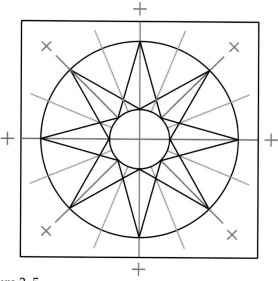

Figure 2–5

DRAFTING THE INTERMEDIATE POINTS

To create the intermediate star points, follow the procedure in the previous step, using only the marks on the eight remaining intermediate gray diagonal lines. Because these intermediate star points are partially hidden behind the large points, it is only necessary to draw the lines from the outer circle to the place where they intersect the major points (Figure 2–6). However, make certain that the straight edge extends precisely from the mark on the outer circle to the appropriate gray mark on the inner circle. With this method, the small star points will have the same angle measurement as the large star points. The

outer setting triangles will be symmetrical, with opposite sides and angles of equal length and measure.

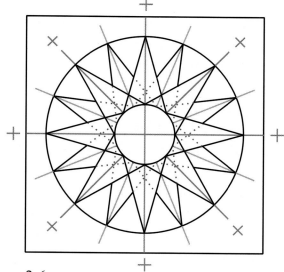

Figure 2–6

REVIEW

Review the steps, making certain that each has been executed accurately. If desired, erase the grid lines (Figure 2–7). The design is now ready for pattern marking and template making, which are discussed in the next chapter. While these step-by-step instructions have resulted in drafting the entire design, it is really only necessary to draw a segment of the design that includes all of

Figure 2–7

the different pattern units. In this case, one-eighth of the design would be sufficient, since each of the pattern units is repeated eight times. Generally, it is necessary to draft only one-fourth, one-fifth, one-sixth, or one-eighth of a circular patchwork design, depending on the characteristics of the individual design.

NUANCES OF DRAFTING CIRCULAR PATCHWORK DESIGNS

Circular designs based on multiples of four appear to be the most common. The first seven designs in the book are drafted according to the steps in the drafting exercise. The variations in these designs are achieved by adding or subtracting lines. For example, an additional concentric circle is added to the Sunburst from Design 5 (Figure 2–8) and Arabian Star from Design 7. The radius of this new circle is determined by the intersection of the legs of the large and intermediate star points. That is, the radius is determined by the existing points of intersection. The additional circle creates a halo effect around the center of the block.

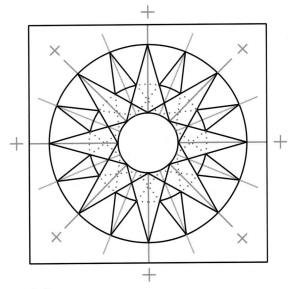

Figure 2–8

Figure 2–9 shows the impact of relating the legs of the smaller star points to a different interi-

or circle (dotted line) that is drawn at an arbitrarily determined radius. In this example, the new circle has a relatively large radius, which results in fatter intermediate points than found in the original design. The adjacent outer triangles are asymmetrical, so half of them need to be cut with a reversed template. The original Slashed Star is shown in Figure 2–7 on page 15, and the new design is Figure 2–9. The new design is a perfectly acceptable variation and, in fact, shows how a quiltmaker might go about creating a new design. The important issue here is an awareness of the impact of relating some design points to an arbitrarily drawn circle rather than all points to the same center circle. A number of designs included in this book make use of arbitrarily chosen radii.

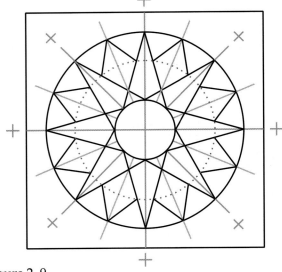

Figure 2–9

By changing only the radius of the interior circle(s), the appearance of a design can be altered while maintaining its basic structure. Figure 2–10 shows a 12-point Single Sunflower design in which the radius of the inner circle is one-fifth the radius of the entire circle; that is, a 1-inch radius center for a 5-inch radius design. Notice the slender shape of the points. On the other hand, the Single Sunflower from Design 12, shown in Figure 2–11, has a center radius that is two-fifths the radius of the entire design. This circle is twice as large as that of Figure 2–10 and the points are much fatter. So, while the structure of both designs is identical, the appearance is somewhat different, because the radii of the inner circles are different.

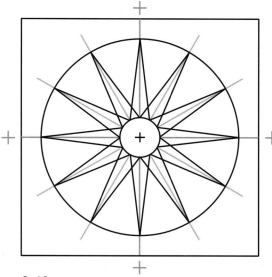

Figure 2–10

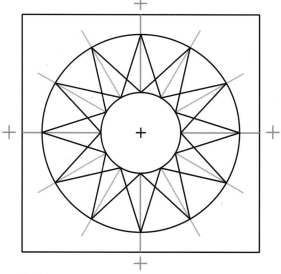

Figure 2–11

Yet another way to change the appearance of a design is to change the number of points. For example, change from a multiple of six to a multiple of five. Figure 2–12 uses the same radii as Figure 2–11, but has 10 points rather than 12. Because there are fewer points for the same 360° circle, each point is fatter. If the design were

changed to 16 points, each point would be more slender.

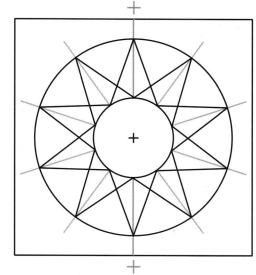

Figure 2–12

The Slashed Star used in the drafting exercise, the Sunburst (Figure 2–8), and Single Sunflower designs (Figures 2–10, 2–11, 2–12) represent a drafting situation in which all the points relate to the inner circle. As noted earlier, this is not always the case. The 12-point Sunflower from Design 9 (Figure 2–13) requires an intermediate circle (dotted line) that is located midway between the outer and inner circles. This intermediate circle is not visible in the completed

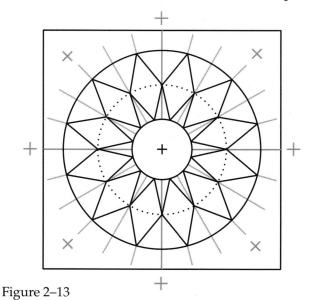

Figure 2–13

design, but it is critical in determining the location and length of the sides of the diamonds. Notice that, while these diamond shapes appear to have four sides of equal length, the legs and angles that touch the outer circle have slightly different measurements than the legs and angles that touch the center circle. The opposite smaller angles and sides are similar but not identical, so extra care must be taken in the preparation and assembly to ensure the correct orientation of this patch. Otherwise, the block will be distorted.

The Sunbirds block from Design 16 (Figure 2–14) requires 24 divisions and an intermediate circle (dotted line) that is used to locate the leading point of the Flying Geese triangles. While these triangles appear to be symmetrical right triangles, there are actually small differences in the measurements of the two short sides and the two small angles, so extra care must be taken to keep the shape correctly oriented.

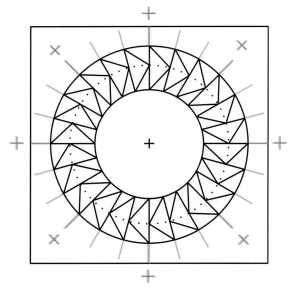

Figure 2–14

The Rising Sun block from Design 15 (Figure 2–15) has a curved unit that spirals out from the center. This feature is somewhat rare in circular patchwork designs, but it can also be found in the Feathered Star block in Design 14. Notice that the long, curved sides of the spiral shapes start and end at a mark on the dashed grid lines. The easiest way to accomplish this manually is to use a curved object such as a plate or a French curve tool. Be careful to use exactly the same curved segment for each of the lines.

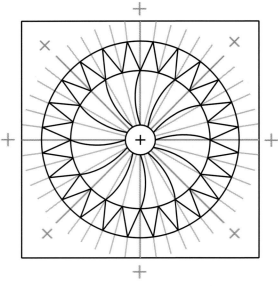

Figure 2–15

Figure 2–15 also shows a straightforward method for drafting a ring of triangles with legs that touch but do not overlap. Designs 11, 13, and 14 have similar rings around the outside edge of the circle. Because the legs touch the circle on different projecting lines than do the points, these designs require twice as many grid lines as the total number of points. For example, the Rising Sun design has 24 points but requires 48 lines for drafting.

CHANGING THE OVERALL SIZE OF A CIRCULAR DESIGN

This chapter has outlined the benefits of learning to draft circular patchwork designs so they can be drawn in any size, whether larger or smaller than the original. The radii for traditional designs are relatively well-established, although they can be varied as described in Figures 2–9, 2–10, and 2–11. In these variations, the overall size of the block remained the same while the proportions changed.

To change the overall size of the block while maintaining the original proportions, some simple math is required to determine the new radii for the circles. Begin with the radius information for 12-inch blocks with 10-inch circular designs, which is provided in Chapter 4 for each of the designs in this book. For example, consider the Slashed Star design from the drafting exercise. The 10-inch design has circles with radii of 1½" and 5". Assume that a 17" circular design is desired instead. The 17" circular design is 1.7 times larger than the original 10-inch circular design (17" ÷ 10" = 1.7). So, the radius of the inner circle must be 1.7 times the original radius, or 1.5" x 1.7 = 2.55". Since 2.55" is slightly less than 2⁹⁄₁₆", rounding it to 2½" is fine. The radius of the outer circle is 5" x 1.7, or 8½".

To illustrate reducing the size of the block, we'll use the Sunbirds design (Figure 2–14), which has circle radii of 2¾", 4", and 5". Assume that a 10" block with a 9" circular design is desired. The 9" circular design is .9 times the size of the original 10" circular design (9" ÷ 10" = .9). So, the radius of the new inner circle is 2.75" x .9 = 2.475". The middle circle is 4" x .9 = 3.6", and the radius of the outer circle is 5" x .9 = 4.5". These numbers can be rounded to the nearest fractions, i.e., 2½", 3⅝", 4½", and the visual effect will be virtually the same as the original.

SETTING SQUARES AND BORDERS

For the setting blocks, the underlying geometric structure of the design is categorized according to the number of major and minor divisions. This information is applied to a grid of squares. The major block categories are four-patch, five-patch, seven-patch, and nine-patch,

and most quilt patterns relate to one of these categories. In fact, with one exception, all of the setting blocks in this book are from the two most common categories: four-patch and nine-patch. Since grid squares of any size can be used, the pattern itself can be easily drafted to any size. It is simply a matter of dividing the desired size square by the number of grid squares in each block. The grid method for drafting the setting blocks is briefly illustrated with two examples. Best of All (Figure 2–16) is a nine-patch design made up of 36 squares; i.e., 6 x 6. If each grid square is 2", the finished block is a 12" square. If a 16" square block is desired, each grid square must be 2⅔". That is, 16" ÷ 6 = 2.6666 or 2⅔".

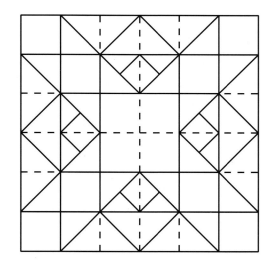

Figure 2–16

Shaded Crossroad (Figure 2–17) is a four-patch design made up of 64 squares; i.e., 8 x 8. If each grid square is 1½", the finished block is a 12" square. If a 16" square block is desired, each grid square must be 2", (16" ÷ 8 = 2"). Because it can be much easier to draw a grid of 2" squares than it is to draw a grid of 2⅔" squares, this second design might be a better choice for a 16" block. On the other hand, for a 15" finished block, the Best of All design is a good choice because it requires a grid of 2½" squares (15" ÷ 6 = 2.5"), while the

Shaded Crossroad design requires a grid of 1⅞" squares (15" ÷ 8 = 1.875").

The same steps are used if a smaller square is desired. For example, for a 10" Best of All block, the grid squares are 1⅔" (10" ÷ 6 = 1.67"), and for a 10" Shaded Crossroad block, the grid squares are 1¼" (10" ÷ 8 = 1.25").

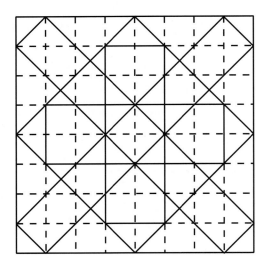

Figure 2–17

Once the size of the grid squares is determined, the grid should be marked on a piece of graph paper. Graph paper is readily available with four, five, six, and eight squares per inch. Match the number of squares per inch to the size of the grid squares. That is, use paper with six squares per inch if the grid squares are 2⅔". Use paper with eight squares per inch if the grid squares are 1⅞", and so on. Draft the block in its new size by methodically connecting appropriate points on the grid. To facilitate pattern drafting, both the block category and number of divisions required for the grid are provided for each of the setting blocks in Chapter 4.

The width of the pieced borders is indicated for each design, too. With this information, it is possible to change the size of the border units using the same basic approach described above. The width of the transition strip (inner border) can be adjusted, if necessary, to ensure that only full units are required for the pieced middle border.

CHAPTER 3

PLANNING AND EXECUTION

The major steps involved in creating a quilt, once the design has been determined, are fabric selection, template making, cutting, assembly, pressing, quilting, and finishing. While these steps are basic to any quilt, the tips and suggestions offered here are intended to ensure that your quilt is both aesthetically and technically successful.

Before purchasing the fabric and cutting the patches for the entire quilt, make a sample consisting of a circular block, a setting block, and a small segment of the border. This allows you to assess the impact of your fabric selections and the accuracy of your template making, cutting, and piecing. It also allows you to determine whether a block is too simple or too complex for your interest level, skills, and available time. Making a sample permits you to determine whether you want to modify the original design by adding or subtracting lines and, thereby, creating more or fewer pattern pieces. Finally, the sample may be used to test pressing plans and quilting designs. Making a sample takes a little extra time, but it is well worth the effort.

FABRIC SELECTION

For function, select fabrics of compatible weight and fiber content, preferably 100 percent cottons, because they are easy to sew and quilt, and they wear consistently well. Before purchasing a fabric, look at the wrong side and ask yourself how well you will be able to see the seam line markings. This is usually a problem when using patterned fabrics, which may be very busy on the back side. If you cannot see marking lines, it is hard to sew straight seams. This problem makes the piecing much more difficult and can have a negative impact on the overall quality of the piecing. With so many fabrics to choose from, you can find an appropriate one that will make the seam line markings easy to see.

For aesthetics, two major considerations go into selecting fabric for a quilt: the color and the motifs in the pattern. Color has three characteristics: hue (the color family), value (the lightness or darkness), and intensity (the brightness or dullness). While quiltmakers may choose to use many different fabrics in their quilts, most quilt designs, including the designs in this book, can be carried out with as few as two or three fabrics if there is adequate value contrast. Value contrast differentiates the figure from the ground. The figure is the recognizable subject matter in the block, such as a star or sunflower. The ground is the remaining background (or left-over space) behind the figure. Just as we are accustomed to reading dark text on a light page, we also may be more comfortable seeing a dark figure on a light background. It comes as no surprise that many quilts have light backgrounds and use more light than dark value fabrics. For variety, you might have a light figure on a dark background. This is called figure-ground reversal and results in a quilt (Design 9) that is generally darker overall in value.

HUE STRATEGIES

There are many ways to choose a color plan for a quilt. The easiest is to begin with a multicolored fabric and then select additional fabrics that complement or match that fabric. While this inspiration fabric will probably be used in the quilt, it does not have to be. The other selected fabrics will still work together. Paintings, decorative art objects, posters, or eye-appealing advertisements may also lend that initial impetus to color selection.

Another approach is to choose a theme and select colors to carry out the theme. Some broad themes are patriotism, nautical, holidays, seasons, countries, continents, or history. Select hues that support the themes, such as, red, white, and blue for patriotism; blue, green, and white for nautical; red, white, and green for Christmas; red, brown, gold, and rust for fall; earth tones and neutrals for North Africa; or strong red, green, blue, and gold for the Renaissance.

A third approach uses the traditional color harmonies of the color wheel. The three most commonly used harmonies are *monochromatic*, *analogous*, and *complementary*. A *monochromatic* plan uses a single hue family, such as a variety of reds. Achromatic colors (black, gray, white) and neutral colors (brown, beige, tan, cream) may also be used with the single hue.

An *analogous* color plan is more varied because it uses a series of hues that are adjacent to each other on the color wheel, such as red, purple, and violet or blue-green, green, and yellow-green.

The *complementary* plan can be the most lively. The hues, which are directly across from each other on the color wheel, not only enhance each other but also exhibit warm and cool contrasts. That is, one complementary hue is always warm and the other is always cool. Examples of complementary color harmonies include red and green, blue and rust, or yellow and violet.

Another approach is to use a wide variety of scraps to execute these quilt designs. Surviving quilts and published designs frequently made use of scraps. When many fabrics are used, it is important to manage the value relationships to emphasize the pieced design. It is also good to distribute the hues throughout the quilt in a way that appears deliberate rather than random. The scraps may be unified by using one fabric consistently in every block, perhaps as the major background fabric.

VALUE CONSIDERATIONS

While quiltmakers generally start by choosing the hues they want to use in a quilt, adequate value contrast is essential. Value is relative, depending on the surrounding fabric. The middle fabrics in Figure 3–1 are dark when compared to the fabrics at the left and light when compared to the fabrics at the right. For a design requiring only two values, either the left and middle fabrics or the middle and right fabrics can be used successfully.

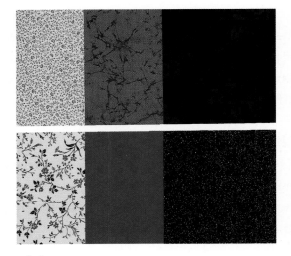

Figure 3–1

If the left and right fabrics are used, the value contrast will be even greater, and the design may appear to be more dynamic.

The impact of different levels of value contrast on a circular design is shown in Figure 3–2. In the left quadrant, the points stand out clearly because of high contrast. In the lower and right quadrants there is a moderate level of contrast, as a result of using light and medium value fabrics the one case and medium and dark value fabrics in another. In the upper quadrant, there is a low level of contrast between the adjacent fabrics. So, the points blend into each other and the background. Contrast need not be high to be effective and low contrast is not always wrong. However, low contrast should be used carefully, where the design calls for adjacent patches to read almost as one, while still maintaining some individuality. The farther the distance from the quilt, the more difficult it is to differentiate patches when a low level of contrast is used.

Figure 3–2

The area of a block that has the highest value contrast with its surroundings will usually become the focal point. So, in a quilt that consists of mostly light values, the dark values will become the focal point. In a quilt that uses a majority of dark fabrics, the light values will become the focal point. It is, therefore, important for the quiltmaker to make deliberate choices about where the highest value contrast occurs.

A reducing glass may be useful in assessing the impact of value placement in blocks. The designs in this book are most effective if the highest value contrast emphasizes the major points of the circular designs and the diagonals in the setting blocks. It is especially important to emphasize the dynamic diagonals of the setting blocks, because they lead the eye across the quilt. Good and poor value placement in a setting block are compared in Figure 3–3. While the same fabrics are used in each block, the good block (left) stretches out energetically while the poor block (right) draws into itself and looks quite static.

Figure 3–3

MANAGING INTENSITY

Once hue and value have been decided, attention should be given to the intensity, the brightness or dullness of a color. In a collection of mostly bright colors, a fabric with dull color appears lifeless. This is especially evident when the colors are of equal value. The brights appear clear and lively, while the dulls look gray and washed out. In a collection of dull-colored fabric, a bright color calls attention to itself, sometimes to the extent that it is distracting, disrupting the unity of the design. Although most very dark colors are also dull, they seem to work with both bright and dull colors of light and medium value. Most dark colors are dull because dark value is achieved by mixing the dyes with black, brown, or the complement, reducing the hue's saturation or intensity. Like hue, intensity is a color characteristic that is affected by trends. Dull intensities are popular for years only to be supplanted by bright colors. Some manufacturers also seem to favor either bright or dull intensity in their fabric lines.

PATTERN MOTIFS IN FABRICS

When patterned fabrics are used, it is important to be aware of the fabric's pattern motifs. Motifs can be categorized according to *value contrast, scale, density, type of shape,* and *pattern placement.* Patterned fabrics with three levels of internal *value contrast* (high, medium, and low) are illustrated in Figure 3–4. Patterns with high internal value contrast can look spotty and be distracting if used in the wrong application. When used in a block, they can blur the edge between patches, which can detract from the design, as illustrated in Figure 3–5. Patterns with low internal contrast often read as solids and are sometimes referred to as *patterned solids.* They are versatile, interesting, and enhance contrast between patches.

Figure 3–5

Three levels of *scale* (large, medium, and small) are shown in Figure 3–6. Assuming the level of internal value contrast in a patterned fabric has been managed, it is more interesting to use fabrics with motifs of several different sizes than to use fabrics that all have the same scale, as shown in Figure 3–7. For a more successful, varied selection of fabrics, see this Sunflower in Design 11 on page 87.

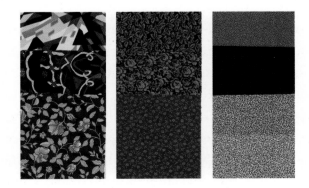

Figure 3–4

Figure 3–6

Figure 3–7

Density refers to how closely the motifs are placed next to each other. Three levels of pattern density (high, medium, and low) are illustrated in Figure 3–8. Using a variety of density levels also adds interest to a quilt.

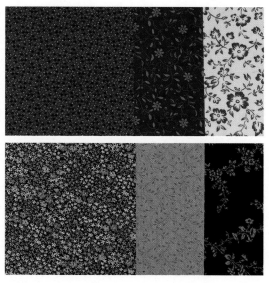

Figure 3–8

Type of shape refers to whether the motifs are derived from nature (flowers and leaves), geometry (squares and circles), or simply invented (blobs and squiggles). More interest is created by using a variety of types of shape, rather than one type.

Pattern placement refers to the order of positioning motifs on the background. The most versatile fabrics have an apparently random placement of motifs. Regularly patterned fabrics (Figure 3–9) have motifs arrayed in an obvious gridlike arrangement. Often, the angle of the grid is arbitrary so, when used in a design, the patches tend to look irregularly shaped and the seams tend to look crooked, even when they are straight. It is generally best to avoid regularly patterned fabrics unless they are needed to achieve a specific look. Stripes, plaids, and other geometric prints are regularly patterned fabrics that can add interest to a quilt. So, the rule of thumb is to use regularly patterned fabrics only for patches that are enhanced by the pattern. Give priority to pattern rather than grainline when cutting the patches. Some regularly patterned fabrics are more subtle than others, so look at the fabric from several angles and at different distances when evaluating it.

Figure 3–9

For miniatures, since many of the patches are very small, special attention must be given to the pattern motifs. For example, a large-scale pattern may look blotchy when cut into small pieces. A low-density pattern may have open areas that appear as solids when used in some patches, while other areas of the same fabric may have a visible pattern. Although there are no hard and fast rules, it is very important to do a mock-up of a miniature block to see how the fabrics work.

Using either all solids or all prints in quilts may result in a more unified look. The availability of patterned solids, low-contrast prints that visually read as solids, makes this easy to do. One solid in a sea of prints, or one print in a sea of solids, tends to call undue attention to the different fabric, which becomes the focal point of the design. The focal point can be created by using value contrast rather than solid versus pattern contrast.

PROPORTION DECISIONS

Once basic decisions have been made about color and pattern motifs, it is still necessary to address proportion, how much of each color (hue, value, intensity) and how much of each type of pattern are desired. Identical quilt designs, made with identical fabrics, can look very different when different amounts of the fabrics are used.

MOCK-UPS

The line drawings for each of the designs on pages 126 – 141 are intended to be used for sample color placement. Establish a preliminary plan. Then, piece samples or create a full-size mock-up of one circular design, one setting block, and a segment of the border. For mock-ups, cut the patches without seam allowances so they fit together well. The interaction of adjacent colors is accurately assessed only when the patches actually touch each other as they will in the finished quilt. Consider using a fusible web, which provides a strong, no-sew bond when activated by a low iron temperature. Fuse the fabrics to one side of the web, cut out the patches, remove the web backing paper, arrange the patches on a piece of muslin or scrap fabric, and fuse them in place. Trim away the excess muslin or scrap fabric. A fabric sample or mock-up is especially convenient for assessing the circular designs, because the circle can be auditioned easily on a variety of different background fabrics (Figure 3–10).

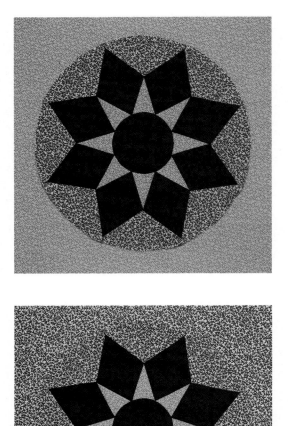

Figure 3–10

To get a better idea of how the circular and setting blocks will look in a whole quilt, it may be helpful to use a multi-faceted lens, which visually replicates the blocks.

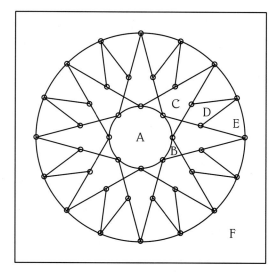

Figure 3–11

TEMPLATE MAKING

Before making templates, analyze the design and note all points where seams intersect. If intersections occur in the middle of a patch rather than at another seam, it is necessary to mark that point on the template, and eventually on the patch. The Slashed Star, shown in Figure 3–11, has 40 such intersections, which are marked with small circles. This is also a good time to mark the grain line on the design, so it can be transferred to the cutting templates. Grain line is discussed later in this chapter. Other information that might be useful to add are the letters identifying the units and the quantities needed.

CUTTING TEMPLATES

Two different sets of templates, one for cutting and one for sewing, are recommended. Cutting templates are made from paper and have a scant ¼" seam allowance (Figure 3–12). Make several sets so they can be replaced if accidentally cut a little

too closely by a scissors or rotary cutter. These paper templates make cutting easy and accurate, as described below.

The pattern pieces for the 12" blocks are too large to fit on the 8½" x 11" pages of this book. One-fourth of each block is provided. Place a paper, folded into fourths, on the dotted lines and mark the solid sewing lines. Cut any partial patch to size and open it up. This is the finished size of the patch. Use this full-size shape to make the templates.

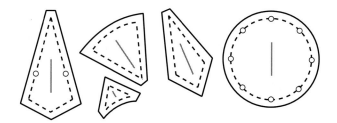

Figure 3–12

Those who are proficient in machine piecing may choose to use only the cutting templates. If so, it is critical that seam allowances on the machine and the template are identical. Furthermore, the corners of the patches and other seam intersections should be marked on these templates. This can be done with a tiny hole punch. Eighth-inch hole punches are available at many office supply stores and are less expensive and easier to find than specialty ¹⁄₁₆" hole punches. Those who piece by hand, or a combination of hand and machine, will need sewing templates as well.

SEWING TEMPLATES

Make a plastic template, without seam allowances, for each different patch in the quilt (Figure 3–13). Carefully trace the shapes onto plastic and add any markings that may be helpful, such as seam intersections, the letter of the template, and the grain line. Cut out the templates. A rotary cutter can be used on straight-sided pieces producing a much truer line than scissors. Double check the templates by placing them on the original patterns and drawing around them with a sharp pencil. Make certain that the drawn lines fall directly on top of the pattern lines. The most common error in making sewing templates is cutting the plastic outside the pencil lines rather than directly on them, resulting in slightly oversized patches that do not fit together precisely.

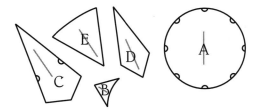

Figure 3–13

TEMPLATES FOR CIRCLES

Since it is difficult to cut accurate circle templates, especially out of plastic, a drafting compass may be used to draw the necessary circles directly on the fabric, eliminating the need for circle templates. This procedure is described in the cutting instructions for circles on page 30.

CUTTING

PREPARATION

Prewash all fabrics. If they are going to bleed, fade, or shrink, let them do it now rather than later. Use spray sizing, spray starch, or liquid starch to add some body to the fabric if needed.

GRAIN LINE

Patches should be cut with attention to fabric grain line (Figure 3–14). The straight of grain runs parallel to the selvage. These threads are the warp of the fabric and, because they were

stretched tightly on the loom, they are the most stable. The cross grain is perpendicular to the selvage, and these threads were woven across the wrap and have more stretch than the straight of grain. True bias is located at a 45° angle to the straight of grain, and has the most give. Ideally, when a quilt is pieced, the straight of grain for all the fabrics runs vertically from top to bottom. This includes the borders, as well. Different grain line orientations appear to absorb and reflect the light differently, so the same fabric can appear to be lighter or darker in value, depending on which direction the grain is running. This is especially visible in solid-color fabrics where the same fabric can look like two different fabrics. If random grain line placement is used in a quilt, it can be visually disruptive to the overall design.

When a quilt includes circular patchwork designs, the convention is for the grain line to radiate outward from the center of the circular block. Figure 3–15 illustrates the desired grain line placement for a circular design, a setting block, and a segment of border. The long lines represent the straight of grain. Notice that when identical shapes have different orientations in the setting block or border, it is necessary to cut like patches with different grain lines. For example, in the setting block, the grain line is parallel to the longest edge of some triangles and perpendicular to the longest edge of others. The same is true of the triangles in the pieced border. When these guidelines are followed, straight of grain is always sewn to straight of grain, cross grain to cross grain, and bias to bias. Because the edges of the patches have the same amount of stretch, there should be no pulling or puckering. Well-constructed quilts that make proper use of grain should hang or lie flat.

One exception to the grain line guidelines

relates to pattern. When regularly patterned fabrics are used, the patches should be cut to work with the pattern even if the pattern is off-grain. With a specialty fabric, such as a border stripe, give priority to letting the stripe enhance the design, even if this requires a variety of grain placements in a block.

To make efficient use of the fabric, cut the plain border strips before cutting the patches. Make certain grain line has been observed, as illustrated in Figure 3–15. Consider cutting the outer border several inches wider than the desired finished size. This allows extra fabric to attach the quilt to the quilting frame. When the quilting has been completed, cut away the excess for a clean, straight edge ready for binding.

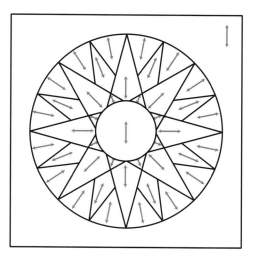

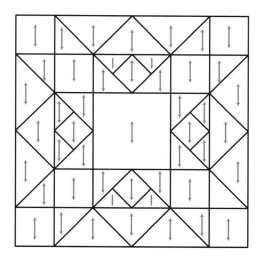

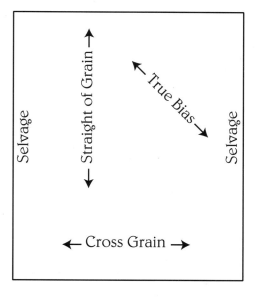

Figure 3–14

STACK CUTTING

It is much faster to stack four layers of fabric, cut the shapes, and mark the seam allowances than it is to use a sewing template to mark four patches on the fabric, add the seam allowances, and cut the patches individually. It also tends to save fabric, since shapes can be butted next to each other. To use the paper cutting template,

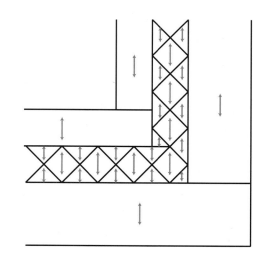

Figure 3–15

stack up to four layers of fabric with the right sides facing up to prevent cutting reversed patches. Next, pin the paper cutting template to the fabric stack, using a needle so there is no pin head to get in the way of a ruler. Make certain the grain line mark on the template matches the straight of grain on the fabric. Lay a ruler over the stack and match the edge of the ruler to the edge of the paper cutting template. Cut out the shape with a rotary cutter. If a shape has a curved edge, it may be easier to cut the curve with scissors after the straight edges have been rotary cut. If you accidentally slice off a little bit of the paper cutting template, the patches should still be fine, at least for hand piecing, because the sewing line will be marked. However, use a new paper cutting template for the next set of patches.

MARKING

Hand piecers, and some machine piecers, rely on marked sewing lines to ensure accurate work. Place the cut shapes wrong side up on a marking surface, such as a piece of aluminum oxide sandpaper, in very fine 220 grade. Use double-stick tape or spray adhesive to adhere two sheets of sandpaper to the inside of a manila file folder for a convenient, portable marking surface. When using sandpaper, it is important not to press so hard that the pencil lead weakens the fabric threads. This can also happen if a coarser grade of sandpaper is used. Most rotary cutting mats also make good marking surfaces. The basic requirement for any marking surface is that it hold the fabric securely in place.

Center the sewing template on the patch so there is a consistent scant ¼" seam allowance on all sides. Mark the sewing line with a very sharp pencil. Mark any intersection points, such as those required for the C unit of the Slashed Star (Figure 3–11, page 27). Also, if patches appear to be symmetrical but are not, as with the petals of the Sunflowers in Designs 8 and 9, make a mark at the tip that touches the center circle. This will make it easier to keep the patches properly oriented, so all the pieces will fit together.

For marking, use a 0.5 mm lead in a mechanical pencil and/or a Berol® Verithin® silver (753) colored pencil. Both are available at office and/or art supply stores. The silver pencil is also sold in quilt shops. Some quiltmakers use other brands and colors of pencils as well. Always test them on a piece of fabric first. Some pencils may leave greasy marks that are hard to remove, while others work very well.

CUTTING CIRCLES

As an alternative to making templates for the background and inner circle, use a drafting compass to mark the circles directly on the fabric. Figure 3–16 illustrates this method with a 10" Slashed Star design set in a 12" square.

First, on the wrong side of a square of background fabric, mark the straight of grain. Then, precisely locate the center of the square. Attach the square, wrong side up, to a firm surface, such as a rotary cutting mat, a dressmaker's cutting board, or a large piece of foam core.

To cut a 10" circle from the background square, extend the radius of the compass to 5". Anchor the compass point at the center of the square of fabric and draw the seam line. Reduce the radius to 4¾" and draw the cutting line.

Next, change the compass radius to 1½" and draw the seam line of the center circle. Increase the radius to 1¾" and draw the cutting line. (The inner circle can be cut from a different fabric, if you prefer).

Before cutting the circles, mark all the intersection points with small circles, as shown in Figure 3–16. This step is important because it ensures that the pieced circle will fit precisely when sewn to the center circle or into the background square. Use the appropriate drafting grid from Appendix A to locate these intersection points. Cut along the cutting lines. If necessary, make small clips in the seam allowances of the background square to facilitate sewing it to the pieced circular design.

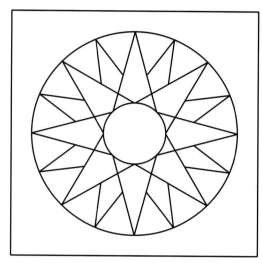

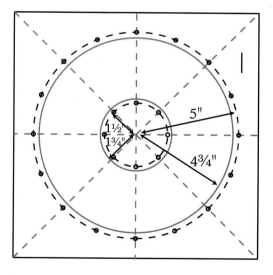

Figure 3–16

Cut the circles carefully on the line. Remember, it's the inner circle and the background corners that will be kept. The "doughnut" shape will be discarded and replaced by the pieced circle.

ASSEMBLY

Before assembling a block, arrange all the pieces on a work board, such as a piece of foam core or cardboard that has been covered with flannel or fleece, so the patches will adhere. The work board should be several inches larger than the blocks, since blocks always take up extra space until the seams are sewn together. To store the work board between sewing sessions, consider using a new pizza box. Pizza boxes come in several sizes, have exactly the right depth, and can usually be purchased inexpensively from stores that sell pizza.

The designs in this book may be pieced by hand or machine, whichever gives the best result. Do not hesitate to use a combination of hand and machine piecing, even in the same block. Choose thread that is compatible with the fabrics and blends with the colors. Keep the stitches small and tight, so they are not pulled apart by the quilting. For hand piecing, use a single knotted thread and backstitch at the beginning, at the end, and every few stitches along the seam. For machine piecing, do not backstitch.

Pinning is important. Use fine silk pins at all the corners and intersections, and at least every inch in between. This close pinning is especially important on curves.

CIRCULAR DESIGNS

Like all patchwork designs, circular designs are pieced in units that become progressively larger. This is clearly illustrated by the piecing diagrams that accompany the designs in Chapter 4. For the most part, piecing begins at the outside and progresses to the center of the block, where the segments are sequentially attached to the center circle if there is one. The circular design, as a unit, is then pieced to the background square. It is important to match the intersection points. Piecing, rather than appliquéing, the circles gives a much better result because the points tend to remain sharper and the circles less distorted. You may want to appliqué the smallest inner circles for the miniature designs, however.

If desired, the background square can be cut slightly oversize. Then, after the circle is set into the background, the square can be trimmed to size, including seam allowances. This larger size provides the opportunity to square-up the block and remove any frayed threads. Before cutting the background square to size, the setting squares should be measured. They should all be the same size, but they may be slightly smaller or larger than the expected 12" or 6", as a result of all the seams. Whatever their final size, cut the background of the circular designs to the same size as the setting blocks. Make certain to cut an equal amount from all four sides so the circle remains centered in the square.

A freezer-paper technique may also be used to piece the circular designs. Instead of preparing plastic sewing templates, cut quantities of freezer paper templates, without seam allowances. Mark intersections where necessary. Then, press the freezer paper templates to the wrong side of the cut shapes. Match and pin at the corners and intersections and sew the patches together along the edge of the freezer paper. If the freezer paper pulls loose from an edge, you can simply press it again to reattach it to the patch. Remove the freezer paper after all sides of a shape have been sewn together.

SETTING BLOCKS

No special piecing techniques are needed for the setting blocks. Strip piecing is also appropriate when a design includes, for example, a four-patch of squares. Many of the designs contain squares made up of half-square triangles for which a grid piecing method for triangles can be used. Extra care should be taken to maintain a consistent vertical grain line on the triangles with any quick-piecing method. First, the grain lines of the two fabrics must run at 90° angles to each other when the fabrics are sewn. When the triangles are cut apart, folded open, and pressed, the grainlines should run in the same direction. Second, attention must be given to the direction of the sewing lines. Sewing from top left to bottom right on a grid of triangles has a different result than sewing from top right to bottom left. When there are many half-square triangles in a design, such as the Kansas Troubles block from Design 9, it is worth taking a few minutes to make up a sample of grid-pieced triangles. Work out the grain line on the sample and then use the technique to make the pieced squares. Quick-piecing methods can save time.

Regardless of the technique used, all the setting blocks should be of identical size when they are completed. Since the circular blocks are trimmed to match, all the blocks will fit together. Consequently, the opposite sides of the quilt should be of equal length, and the seams used to sew the blocks to each other should be straight and parallel to each other.

FOUNDATION PIECING

Foundation piecing has become very popular. It is described only briefly, since there are many books devoted exclusively to the topic. Foundation piecing involves sewing the patches by hand or machine to a fabric, paper, or similar foundation block that has been marked with the design. The technique is frequently used for miniatures, because it has the potential for great precision. However, it can be far more time consuming than conventional piecing, much more difficult to maintain proper grain placement (which is often disregarded), and tedious to remove the backing. Nevertheless, foundation piecing has many devotees, and it is adaptable to a variety of blocks, including larger sizes. Consult the bibliography for books on foundation and other piecing methods.

TIPS FOR MINIATURES

Small blocks require even more attention to precise piecing than do larger blocks. Scant ¼" seam allowances still seem to work best, although it may be necessary to grade them after the seam has been sewn to reduce bulk. It is much easier to hold onto a small patch if it has the standard seam allowance, and fraying is less likely to be a problem. Strip-piecing and grid-piecing techniques make miniatures easier to sew. Some quiltmakers may want to use foundation piecing for the smaller blocks.

BORDERS

Quilts in this book use a combination of plain and pieced borders. The width of each border has been considered carefully so the borders do not overshadow the interior. If a larger or smaller quilt is desired, increase or decrease the number or size of blocks rather than greatly modifying the border dimensions. Before sewing any of the borders to the quilt, assemble the pieced middle border. It may be necessary, because of all the seams, to slightly modify the width of the inner border if the length of the pieced border differs from the original design. Make certain the borders are symmetrical and the corners are identical.

When the necessary adjustments have been made, mark the center of each border strip. Then, mark off intervals that relate to the size of the units in the setting blocks and border. A dressmaker's cutting board, which has a 1" grid, is use-

ful for measuring and marking borders. If the blocks have shrunk or grown a little, make the necessary adjustments so the borders fit the finished size of the blocks. Lay the plain border strips next to each other, so they can all be marked at the same time for consistency. Attach the border strips sequentially, always matching the marks to the seams in the interior of the quilt or in the pieced border. This ensures that the seams do not wobble from side to side or top to bottom throughout the body of the quilt.

PRESSING

Careful pressing using a blocking board is important to the success of a quilt. It is worth taking time to develop a pressing plan for the circular design, the setting block, and a unit of the pieced border. One way to make a blocking and pressing board is by stretching a piece of tightly woven muslin over a piece of cardboard or foam core (slightly larger than the size of the block) and marking the major lines of the block on the fabric. For the 10" circle of the Slashed Star design, for example, the marks on the blocking board include a 5" radius circle with 16 dashes representing the 16 points, and a center mark. These lines are drawn using the same method illustrated in Figure 3–16 on page 31 for marking the background block. For the setting blocks, cover a corner of a dressmaker's cutting board with a piece of muslin, since the 1" markings will show through the muslin.

For hand piecing, sew one entire block before pressing it. Then, lay the block face down on the blocking board and align the seams with the lines on the muslin. Hold the seams in place with pins that are placed perpendicular to the board. For the circular designs, press the seam allowances away from the narrow points, if possible. If it is necessary to reduce the bulk at points, press the seam allowances open. Press the center circle's seam allowances toward the center. Where the circle is set into the background square, press the seam toward the background square. It is usually not necessary to notch these seams to take out fullness unless the circle is very small. For the setting blocks and border units, begin working in the center, fanning the seam allowances so they rotate around intersection points as much as possible. Hold them in place with more perpendicular pins. Having flat intersections is more important than pressing to the dark fabric. Handle the seam allowances in similar sections of a block in a consistent manner.

Once the direction of every seam has been determined, begin pressing at one corner, working slowly and taking out the pins one at a time. Turn the block to the right side and make certain there are no folds in the wells of the seams. If necessary, press again lightly. Trim dog ears (points that stick out beyond the seam allowances) and grade any seam allowances that show through to the front. Having spent all this time establishing a good plan, use it consistently in every block in the quilt. After the first block is complete, you may press seam allowances during the piecing process rather than waiting until the block is complete. Because each block is pressed identically, each looks the same and responds to quilting in the same way. Figure 3–17 illustrates a pressing plan for a circular block. When machine piecing, the pressing plan may be worked out on paper ahead of time. Working with drawings of the blocks and border, draw arrows to indicate the direction seam allowances will be pressed, following the principles of fanning points and reducing bulk as much as possible. Then, apply this paper plan to the blocks as each seam is sewn.

When possible, follow the convention of pressing seam allowances to one side, rather than open. However, do not hesitate to press them open, if necessary, to reduce the bulk. Again, what is most important is the flatness of the finished block.

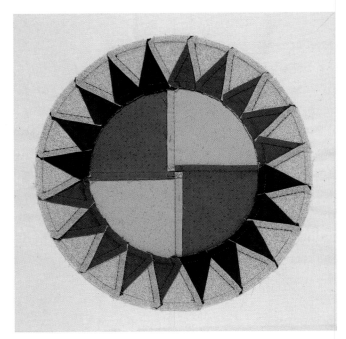

Figure 3–17

QUILTING AND FINISHING

The quilting design is both functional and aesthetic. It holds the fabric sandwich together and reinforces the pieced design. Because the pieced designs in this book are very active, the quilting design can simply highlight the pieced blocks and border. This can be accomplished by a combination of outline and in-the-ditch quilting (in the well of the seam), as well as additional lines that echo the shapes in the blocks. Consider extending the points of the circular designs into the background square to keep the diagonal movement going. The quilting design in the body of the quilt should be visually expansive rather than constraining. The quilting in the inner border can be used to contain the design. Diagonal grids or other linear quilting designs may be used here. Because the outer border is wider, it is suitable for more elaborate quilting, such as cables, feathers, and vines. The sample blocks and border that were recommended at the beginning of this chapter can be used to perfect the quilting design.

A low-loft batting is a good choice because it is easy to quilt through, provides enough relief to show off the quilting design, and is suitable for bed or wall quilts. The relatively flat batting can be used for both traditional and contemporary looks. Always use a quality batting and quilting thread. The thread color should harmonize with the fabrics. Often, a medium-value gray quilting thread can be used on the entire quilt, because it unifies a variety of hues and values, contrasting equally with the light and dark values and blending with the medium values.

The binding should enhance, rather than detract from, what is already happening in the quilt. Matching it to the final border is appropriate. A high contrast between the final border and the binding is likely to call excessive attention to the binding. Regularly patterned fabrics are usually not a good choice, because they may make the binding look twisted or crooked even when it is not. At the same time, a subtle stripe or plaid cut on the bias can be attractive if it relates to fabrics used elsewhere in the quilt.

Use a French or double binding that is cut either on-grain or on the bias. The width of the binding fabric should be six times the desired finished width plus approximately ¼" which is taken up in the folds. For a ¼" finished binding, cut the strips 1¾" wide. Sew strips together, making a length to fit the perimeter of the quilt plus a little extra. Fold the binding strip in half with wrong sides together and press. Stitch the bind-

ing to the front of the quilt with a scant ¼" seam allowance. Fold it to the back so it covers the first stitching line, and stitch along the fold by hand, using a small blindstitch. Sew the corner miters closed. If the quilt is to be hung, adding a 4" sleeve is customary. The sleeve will be unobtrusive if it matches the backing fabric.

Name, date, and sign the quilt. One easy way to record this information is to type it on a piece of fabric. Heat set the typed label with a dry iron and appliqué the fabric label to the backing, usually at a bottom corner.

NOTES

• Cutting requirements are included to make one block.

• Dotted lines on the line drawings show the portion of the block included as the full-size pattern.

• The templates provided in Chapter 4 do not have seam allowances. If you mark the seam lines for hand piecing, remember to add ¼" seam allowances when cutting out the patches. Or, use the cutting template approach discussed on page 27.

• If you use a rotary cutter, you may prefer to add the ¼" seam allowances to the templates so you do not have to remember to add them while cutting. See page 27 for an explanation.

CHAPTER 4

DESIGNS

The 16 circular, setting block, and border designs that follow are arranged according to the circular design categories discussed in the first chapter. The first seven designs have compass/star pictorial characteristics. The next five have sunflower/sun characteristics, and the final four designs are miscellaneous. When classified according to structure, the first ten designs are based on multiples of four and have eight or 16 points. Only Design 11, which has 20 points, is based on a multiple of five. The remaining designs are based on multiples of six and have either 12 or 24 points.

Four guidelines prompted the circular design, setting block, and border combinations. First, the total number of patches in the circular and setting blocks is similar. Second, the relative size of the patches in the circular and setting blocks is somewhat similar. Third, there is some visual relationship between the shapes in the circular design and those in the setting block. Finally, the shape(s) in the border relate to the shapes in the circular and/or setting blocks.

If a pattern piece for a 12" block is too large to fit on the 8½" x 11" pages of this book, one-half or one-fourth of the shape is provided. Draw out the full shape to make a full-size pattern.

For each of the 16 quilts, the following is provided:

- A general history of the designs used in the quilt
- Small drawings keyed to the block and border templates
- Basic drafting and construction information for the circular and setting blocks
- Piecing diagrams for the circular and setting blocks, with values added to the designs
- One-quarter, or more, of the 12" circular and setting blocks
- Border templates for the full-size and miniature pieced borders and dimensions for the other plain borders
- A line drawing of a 35-block, bordered quilt, suitable for testing out color strategies (see pages 126 – 141)
- Six-inch circular and setting blocks keyed to the template information (see pages 142 – 157)

These designs are provided as a departure point. Feel free to modify them as you like. For more block ideas, see the bibliography.

Patterns and quilt layouts provided in this book may be copied for personal use only.

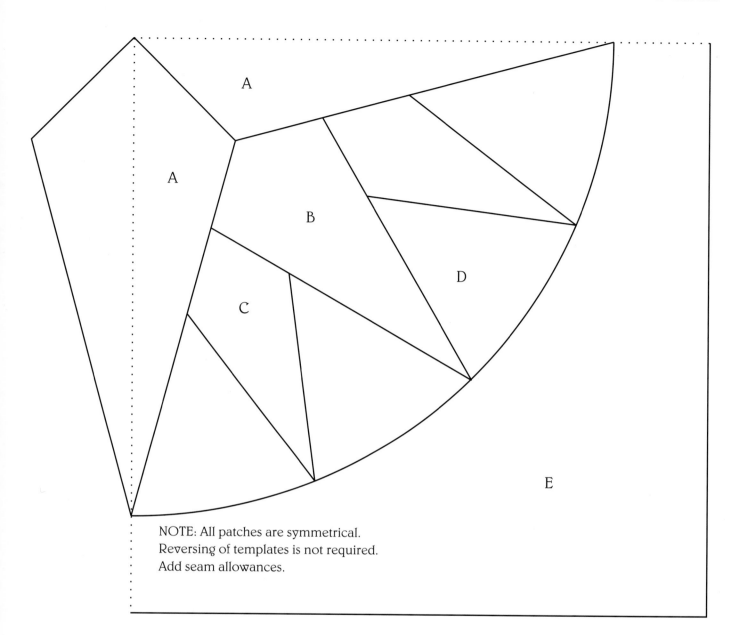

NOTE: All patches are symmetrical.
Reversing of templates is not required.
Add seam allowances.

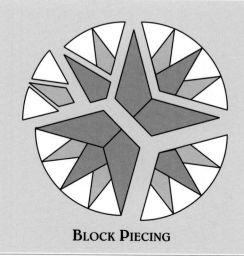

BLOCK PIECING

MARINER'S COMPASS

DRAFTING AND CONSTRUCTION REQUIREMENTS

Number of points: 16
Number of divisions: 16

RADIUS OF CIRCLES

For 12" block: 1½", 5"
For 6" block: ¾", 2½"
Total number of patches: 33

CUTTING REQUIREMENTS

A – 4
B – 4
C – 8
D – 16
E – 1

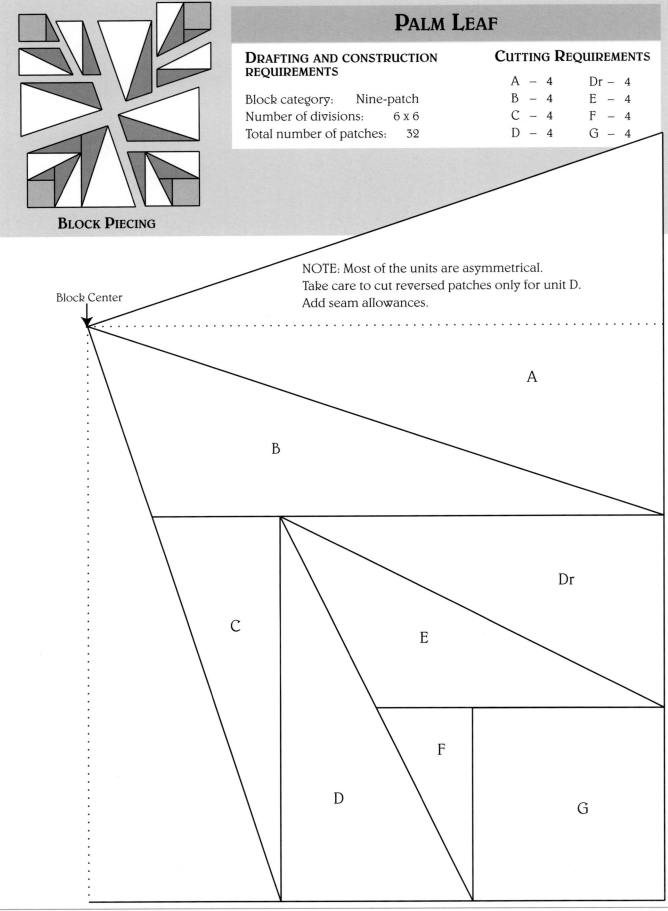

BLOCK PIECING

PALM LEAF

DRAFTING AND CONSTRUCTION REQUIREMENTS

Block category:	Nine-patch
Number of divisions:	6 x 6
Total number of patches:	32

CUTTING REQUIREMENTS

A	– 4	Dr	– 4
B	– 4	E	– 4
C	– 4	F	– 4
D	– 4	G	– 4

NOTE: Most of the units are asymmetrical.
Take care to cut reversed patches only for unit D.
Add seam allowances.

Block Center

A

B

Dr

C

E

F

D

G

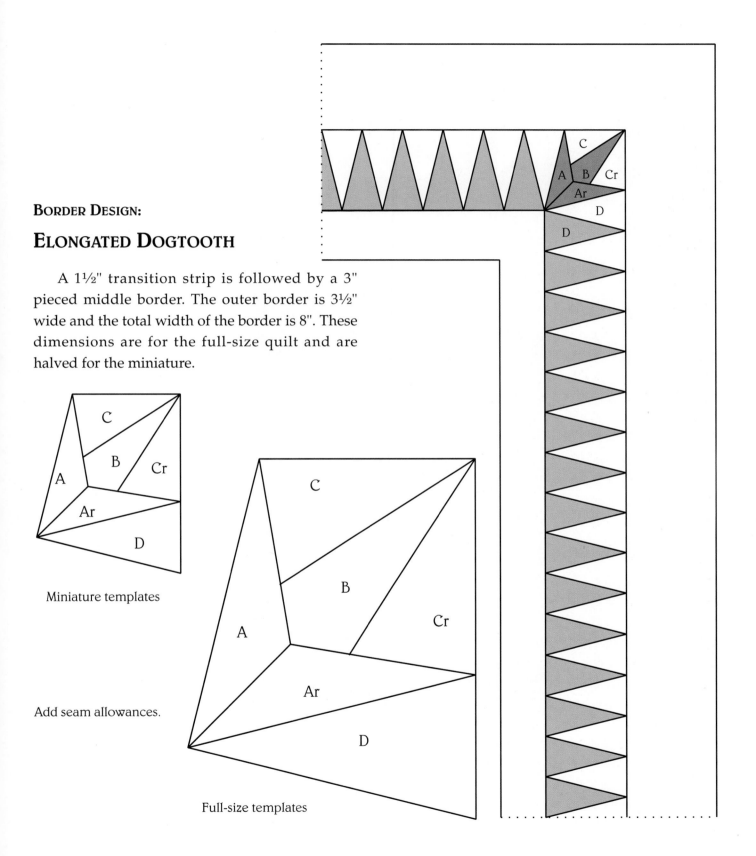

BORDER DESIGN:

ELONGATED DOGTOOTH

A 1½" transition strip is followed by a 3" pieced middle border. The outer border is 3½" wide and the total width of the border is 8". These dimensions are for the full-size quilt and are halved for the miniature.

Miniature templates

Add seam allowances.

Full-size templates

For a line drawing of this quilt, see page 126.

DESIGN 2

BALTIMORE BELLE

MARINER'S COMPASS

SPLIT SQUARES BORDER

CIRCLE DESIGN:

MARINER'S COMPASS

Several mid-nineteenth century quilts utilized this Mariner's Compass block. A quilt by Mary Canfield Benedict (c. 1850) used red and blue stars on a white background. The blocks of this Vermont quilt, now in The Shelburne Museum, are separated by a blue and red Garden Maze sashing. A New England quilt from 1855–1865 executes this design in red and white compass points surrounded by green triangles. The circles are set on a white ground, and the quilt is embellished with appliquéd flowers between the compasses and a border of appliquéd red and green leaves.

The fabrics for the split points may be strip-pieced prior to cutting. Then construct the block in the same manner as Design 1.

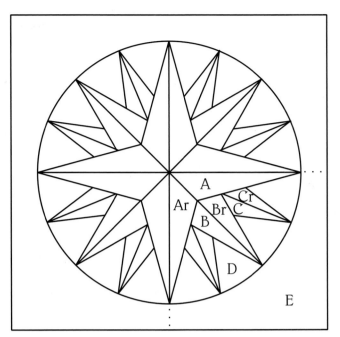

Mariner's Compass

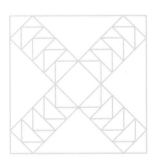

SETTING BLOCK DESIGN:

BALTIMORE BELLE

The Baltimore Belle design was published in a 1906 collection of quilt patterns. It also appeared in the early twentieth century with the name Wild Goose Chase.

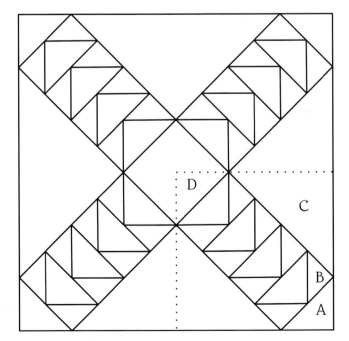

Baltimore Belle

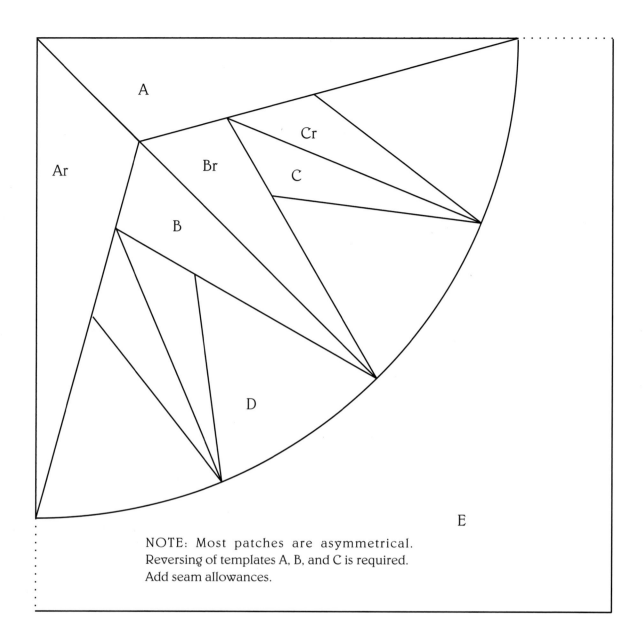

NOTE: Most patches are asymmetrical.
Reversing of templates A, B, and C is required.
Add seam allowances.

BLOCK PIECING

MARINER'S COMPASS

DRAFTING AND CONSTRUCTION REQUIREMENTS

Number of points: 16
Number of divisions: 16

RADIUS OF CIRCLES

For 12" block: 1½", 5"
For 6" block: ¾", 2½"
Total number of patches: 49

CUTTING REQUIREMENTS

A – 4
Ar – 4
B – 4
Br – 4
C – 8
Cr – 8
D – 16
E – 1

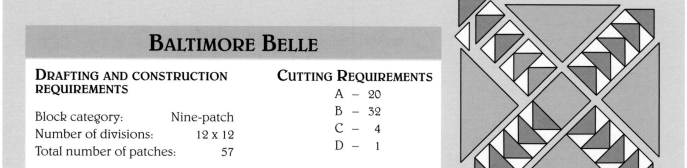

BALTIMORE BELLE

DRAFTING AND CONSTRUCTION REQUIREMENTS

Block category: Nine-patch
Number of divisions: 12 x 12
Total number of patches: 57

CUTTING REQUIREMENTS

A – 20
B – 32
C –   4
D –   1

BLOCK PIECING

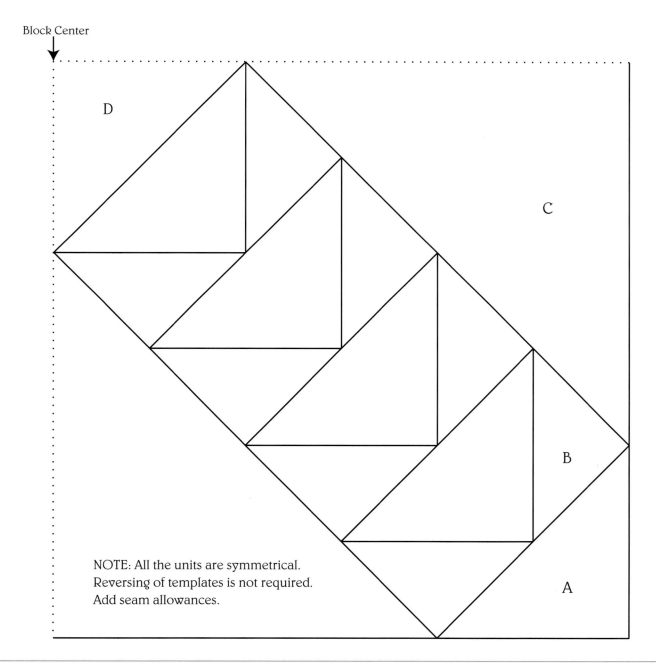

Block Center

D

C

B

A

NOTE: All the units are symmetrical.
Reversing of templates is not required.
Add seam allowances.

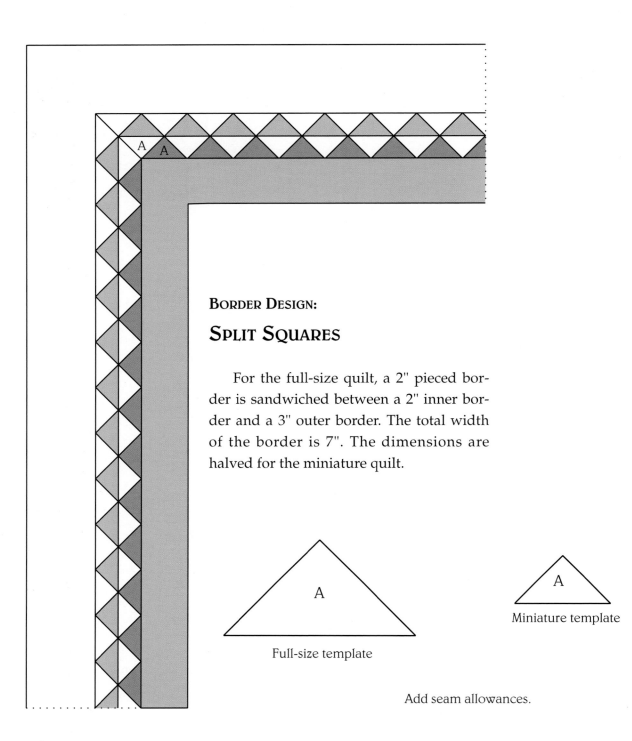

Border Design:

Split Squares

For the full-size quilt, a 2" pieced border is sandwiched between a 2" inner border and a 3" outer border. The total width
of the border is 7". The dimensions are
halved for the miniature quilt.

Full-size template

Miniature template

Add seam allowances.

For a line drawing of this quilt, see page 127.

DESIGN 3

STAR
AND
CROSS

MARINER'S
COMPASS

SQUARES ON
POINT
BORDER

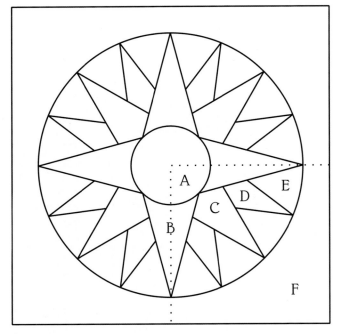

Mariner's Compass

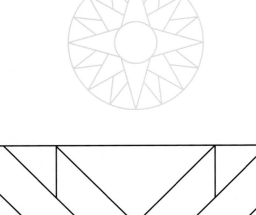

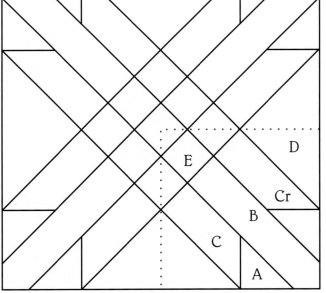

Star and Cross

CIRCLE DESIGN:

MARINER'S COMPASS

This Mariner's Compass design is distinguished by the lack of small triangles around the center circle, as found in Design 4. Nineteenth century quilts using 20-, 24-, 32-, 40-, and 48-point versions of this basic design are found in many states including Massachusetts, New York, Vermont, Pennsylvania, New Jersey, Kentucky, Indiana, Texas, and Minnesota. In twentieth century publications, the 32-point version is also identied as Sunburst, Chips and Whetstones, and The Explosion. Block-to-block and sashed settings are most commonplace in these quilts. However, two extraordinarily handsome quilts from the last half of the nineteenth century combine this block with an appliquéd Princess Feather setting and a floral vine border. See the quilt on page 7.

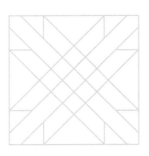

SETTING BLOCK DESIGN:

STAR AND CROSS

In the late 1890s, Ladies Art Company offered the Star and Cross design through its mail-order pattern service. It was published during the second quarter of the twentieth century under the names North Star and Shining Hour. A similar design, which has five rather than nine small squares at the center, is called Mexican Star, Mexican Rose, or Panama Block.

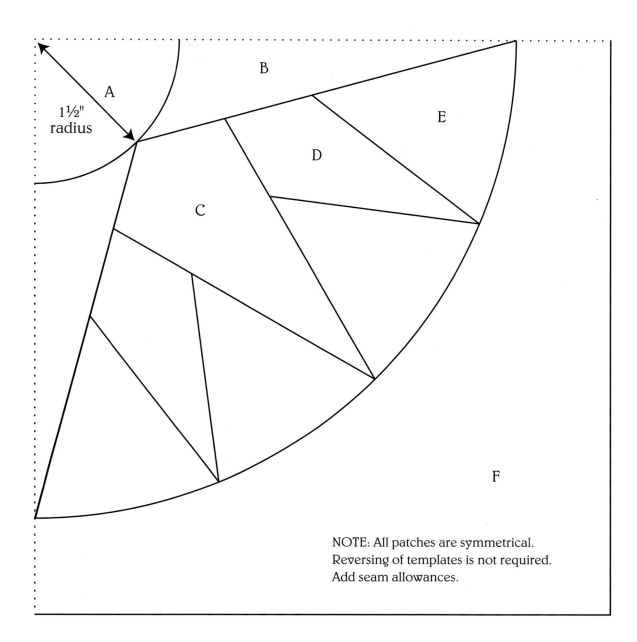

1½"
radius

A

B

D

E

C

F

NOTE: All patches are symmetrical.
Reversing of templates is not required.
Add seam allowances.

BLOCK PIECING

MARINER'S COMPASS

DRAFTING AND CONSTRUCTION REQUIREMENTS

Number of points:	16
Number of divisions:	16

RADIUS OF CIRCLES

For 12" block:	1½", 5"
For 6" block:	¾", 2½"
Total number of patches:	34

CUTTING REQUIREMENTS

A – 1
B – 4
C – 4
D – 8
E – 16
F – 1

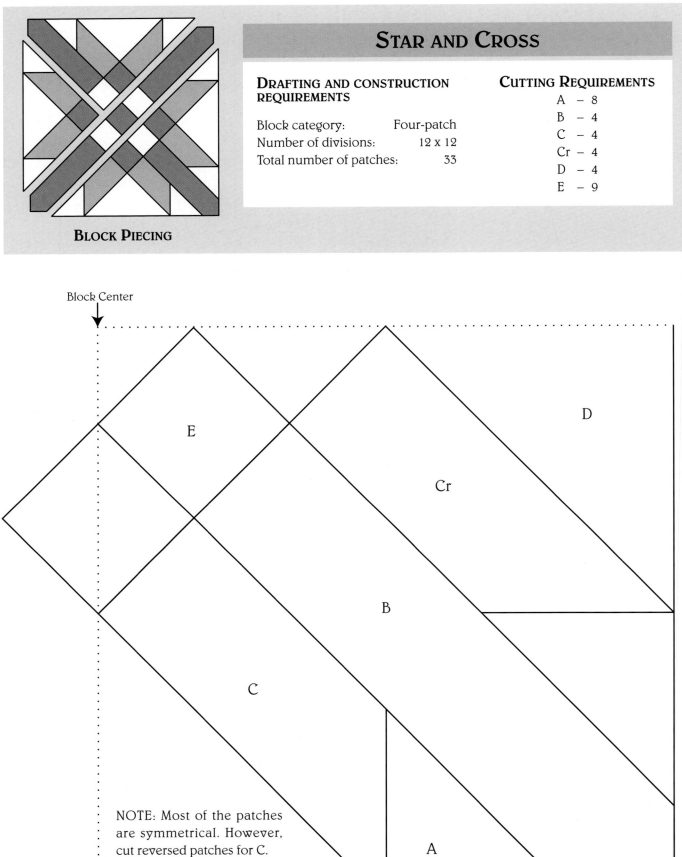

STAR AND CROSS

BLOCK PIECING

DRAFTING AND CONSTRUCTION REQUIREMENTS

Block category:	Four-patch
Number of divisions:	12 x 12
Total number of patches:	33

CUTTING REQUIREMENTS

A	– 8
B	– 4
C	– 4
Cr	– 4
D	– 4
E	– 9

Block Center

D

E

Cr

B

C

A

NOTE: Most of the patches are symmetrical. However, cut reversed patches for C. Add seam allowances.

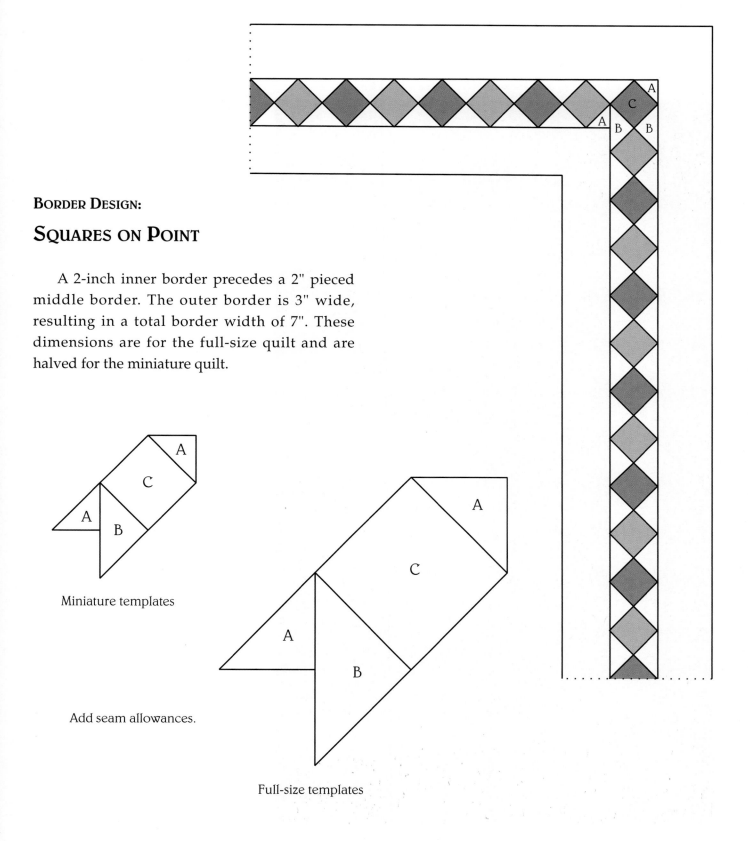

BORDER DESIGN:

SQUARES ON POINT

A 2-inch inner border precedes a 2" pieced middle border. The outer border is 3" wide, resulting in a total border width of 7". These dimensions are for the full-size quilt and are halved for the miniature quilt.

Miniature templates

Add seam allowances.

Full-size templates

For a line drawing of this quilt, see page 128.

DESIGN 4

BEST OF ALL

SLASHED STAR

SHADED SAWTOOTH BORDER

CIRCLE DESIGN:

SLASHED STAR

Slashed Star is a compass-type design characterized by a center circle that is surrounded by small triangles. Several nineteenth century New England quilts utilize the 32-point or 48-point versions of the design, while an 1840s Baltimore Album quilt includes a 24-point block. Beginning in the late 1890s the Ladies Art Company published a 48-point, 24" diameter version that was one of their most expensive designs. In 1935, Carrie Hall identified the design as Sunflower and noted that it had been very popular in the early nineteenth century. She recommended executing it in brown and yellow. In 1949, Marguerite Ickis suggested appliqué as the construction technique for the same design. Alternate names for the design also include Blazing Sun, Blazing Star, Mariner's Compass, and Chips and Whetstones.

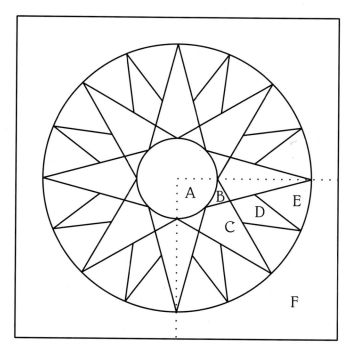

Slashed Star

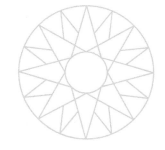

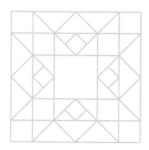

SETTING BLOCK DESIGN:

BEST OF ALL

In 1906, this design was published under the name Best of All. It was called Christmas Star when it appeared in the magazine *Workbasket* in 1950.

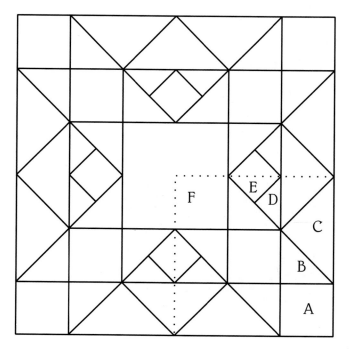

Best of All

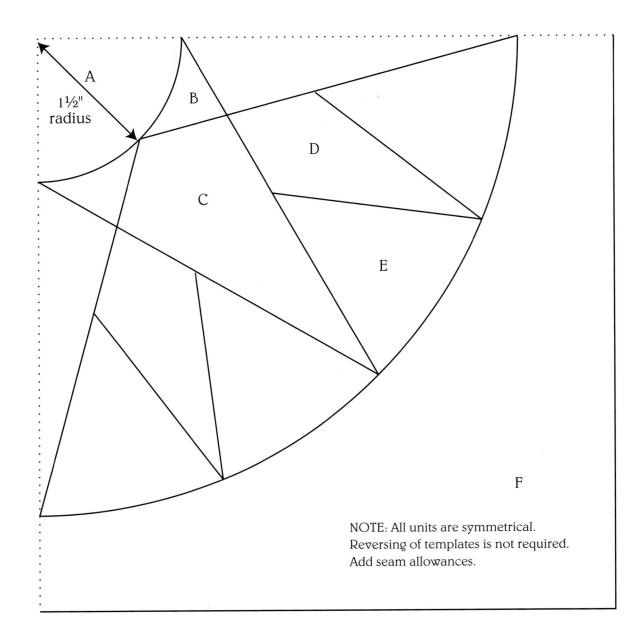

A

1½" radius

B

D

C

E

F

NOTE: All units are symmetrical.
Reversing of templates is not required.
Add seam allowances.

BLOCK PIECING

SLASHED STAR

DRAFTING AND CONSTRUCTION REQUIREMENTS

Number of points:	16
Number of divisions:	16

RADIUS OF CIRCLES

For 12" block:	1½", 5"
For 6" block:	¾", 2½"
Total number of patches:	42

CUTTING REQUIREMENTS

A –	1
B –	8
C –	8
D –	8
E –	16
F –	1

BLOCK PIECING

BEST OF ALL

DRAFTING AND CONSTRUCTION REQUIREMENTS

Block category: Nine-patch
Number of divisions: 6 x 6
Total number of patches: 49

NOTE: All units are symmetrical.
Reversing of templates is not necessary.
Add seam allowances.

CUTTING REQUIREMENTS

A – 8
B – 16
C – 12
D – 8
E – 4
F – 1

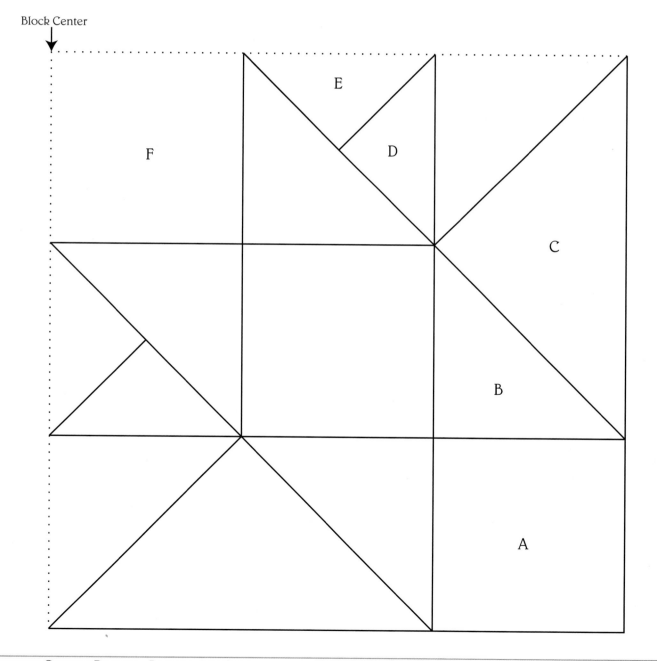

Block Center

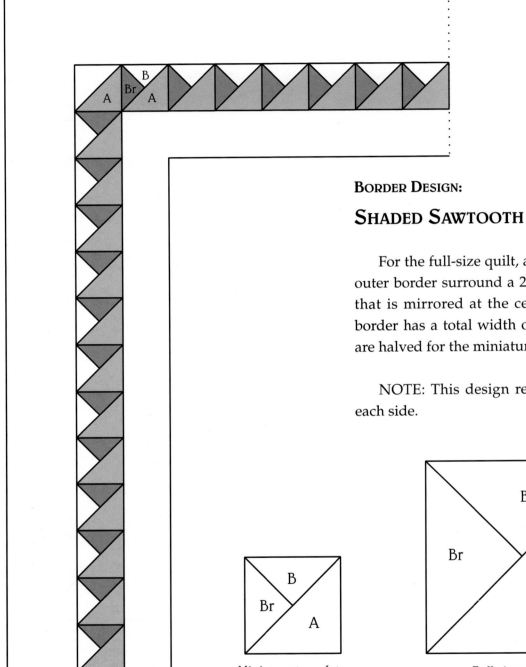

Border Design:

Shaded Sawtooth

For the full-size quilt, a 2" inner border and 3" outer border surround a 2" pieced middle border that is mirrored at the center of each side. The border has a total width of 7". These dimensions are halved for the miniature quilt.

NOTE: This design reverses at the center of each side.

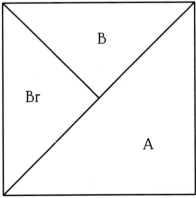

Miniature templates   Full-size templates

Add seam allowances.

For a line drawing of this quilt, see page 129.

BLACKFORD'S BEAUTY

SUNBURST

SUNBEAMS BORDER

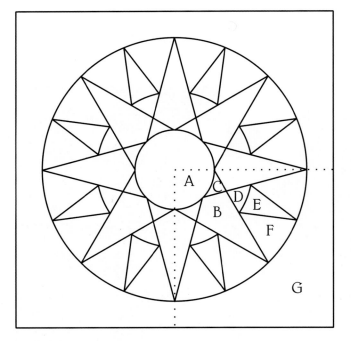

Sunburst

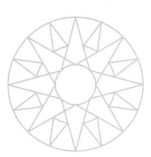

CIRCLE DESIGN:

SUNBURST

A 32-point version of this Sunburst design appeared in *Ladies' Home Journal* in the early twentieth century. A 24-point version, which dates to the early nineteenth century, can be found in The Shelburne Museum. The Smithsonian houses a mid-nineteenth century red and white Sunburst with 20 points. The pattern for the Smithsonian quilt was published in *Museum Quilts*, a booklet that was available in the 1960s from Old Chelsea Needlecraft Service. Other early names for the block include Blazing Sun, Harvest Sun, Rising Sun, Sunbeam, and Sunshine. Today, it is also called Mariner's Compass.

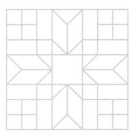

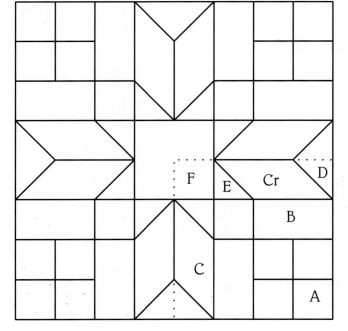

Blackford's Beauty

SETTING BLOCK DESIGN:

BLACKFORD'S BEAUTY

Blackford's Beauty was published by the Ladies Art Company in the late 1890s. About 1910, it appeared in *Needlecraft Magazine* as Good Cheer, while in 1920, *Farmer's Wife* called it Arrowhead. Its other colorful names included The Hunt, Black Beauty, Star and Stripe, Stepping Stones, and Mrs. Smith's Favorite. Many of these names date to the 1930s when the design was published widely.

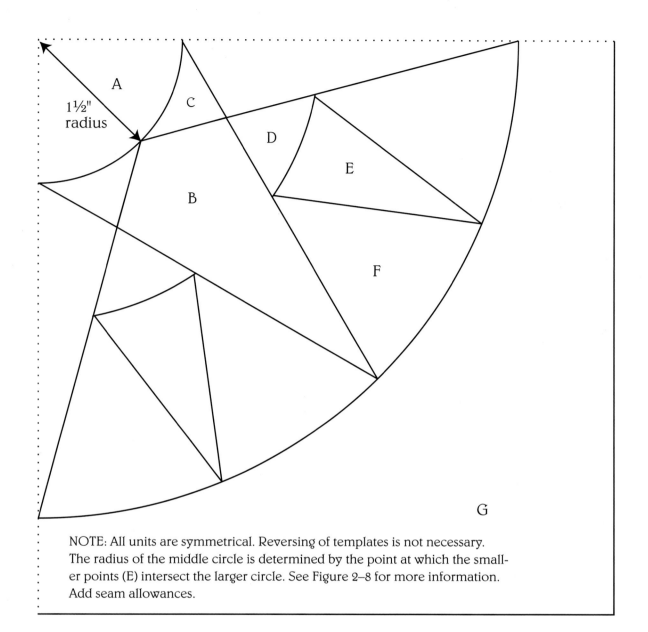

1½"
radius

A

C

D

E

B

F

G

NOTE: All units are symmetrical. Reversing of templates is not necessary.
The radius of the middle circle is determined by the point at which the small-
er points (E) intersect the larger circle. See Figure 2–8 for more information.
Add seam allowances.

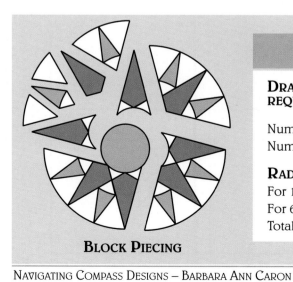

BLOCK PIECING

SUNBURST

DRAFTING AND CONSTRUCTION REQUIREMENTS		CUTTING REQUIREMENTS	
		A –	1
Number of points:	16	B –	8
Number of divisions:	16	C –	8
		D –	8
RADIUS OF CIRCLES		E –	8
For 12" block:	1½", 5"	F –	16
For 6" block:	¾", 2½"	G –	1
Total number of patches:	50		

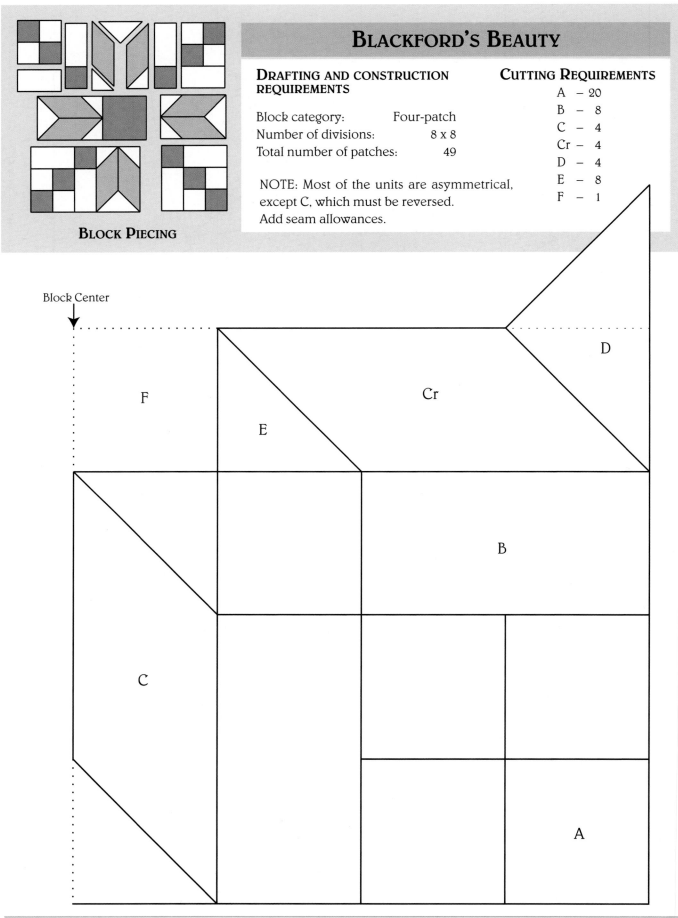

BLOCK PIECING

BLACKFORD'S BEAUTY

DRAFTING AND CONSTRUCTION REQUIREMENTS

Block category: Four-patch
Number of divisions: 8 x 8
Total number of patches: 49

NOTE: Most of the units are asymmetrical, except C, which must be reversed.
Add seam allowances.

CUTTING REQUIREMENTS

A – 20
B – 8
C – 4
Cr – 4
D – 4
E – 8
F – 1

Block Center

F

D

Cr

E

C

B

A

BORDER DESIGN:

SUNBEAMS

For the full-size quilt, a 1½" inner border and a 3½" outer border sandwich a 3" pieced border of sunbeams and triangles. The total width of the border is 8". For the miniature quilt, the borders are one-half these dimensions.

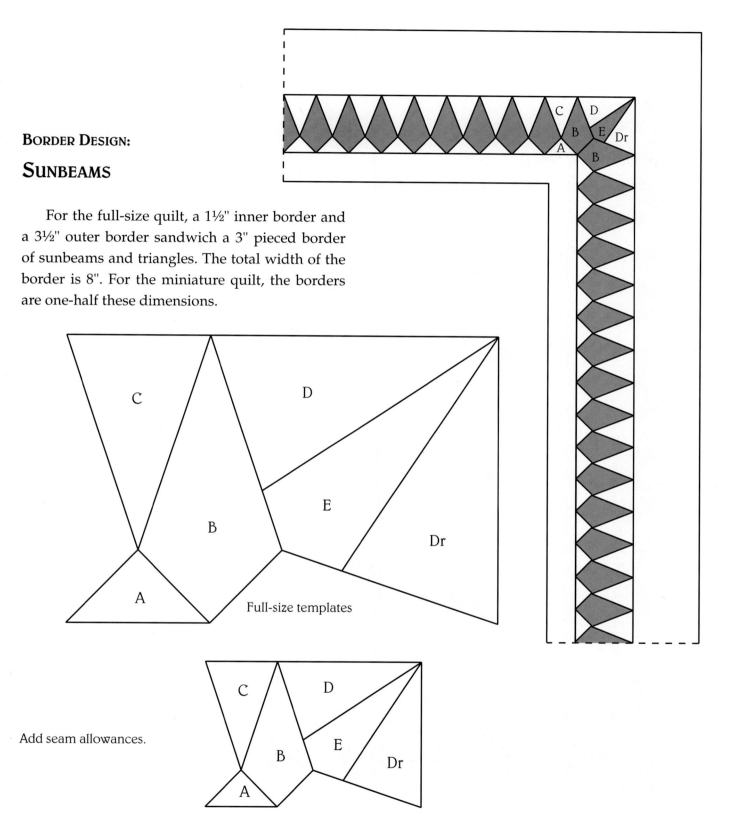

Full-size templates

Add seam allowances.

Miniature templates

For a line drawing of this quilt, see page 130.

DESIGN 6

AMISH STAR

CHIPS AND WHETSTONES

DOGTOOTH AND SPLIT SQUARES BORDER

CIRCLE DESIGN:

CHIPS AND WHETSTONES

Chips and Whetstones is the name most commonly associated with the 32-point version of this design, which was published in *The Kansas City Star* in 1931. Carrie Hall illustrated it in 1935, noting that it was a very old pattern with several names "but none so quaint as this." A whetstone is a tapered tool used to sharpen tools including axes. Chips probably refers to the woodchips that resulted from using the sharpened tool to cut up trees.

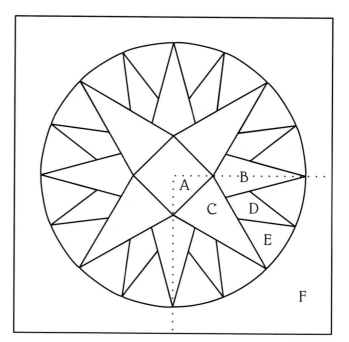

Chips and Whetstones

SETTING BLOCK DESIGN:

AMISH STAR

This block takes its name from an Ohio Amish quilt (c. 1930). Note that the traditional Sawtooth Star, for which a published pattern was available by the mid-1880s, can be found in the center 16 squares. Furthermore, patterns based on a single quadrant (quarter) of the design were published in 1933 as Double Hour Glass and in 1941 as Contrary Wife. Quadrilateral repetition of that smaller block results in this star design.

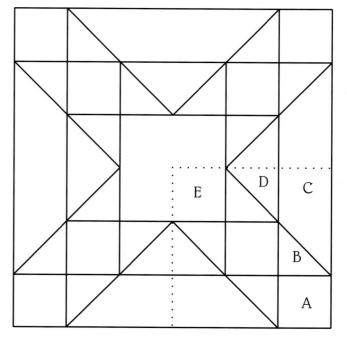

Amish Star

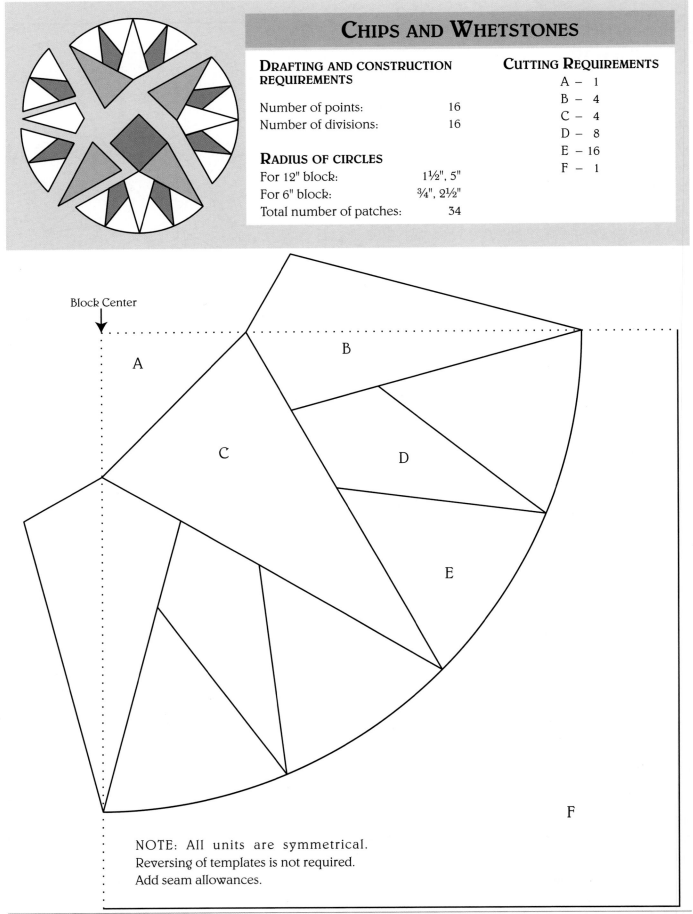

CHIPS AND WHETSTONES

DRAFTING AND CONSTRUCTION REQUIREMENTS

Number of points: 16
Number of divisions: 16

RADIUS OF CIRCLES

For 12" block: 1½", 5"
For 6" block: ¾", 2½"
Total number of patches: 34

CUTTING REQUIREMENTS

A – 1
B – 4
C – 4
D – 8
E – 16
F – 1

Block Center

A

B

C

D

E

F

NOTE: All units are symmetrical.
Reversing of templates is not required.
Add seam allowances.

Block Center

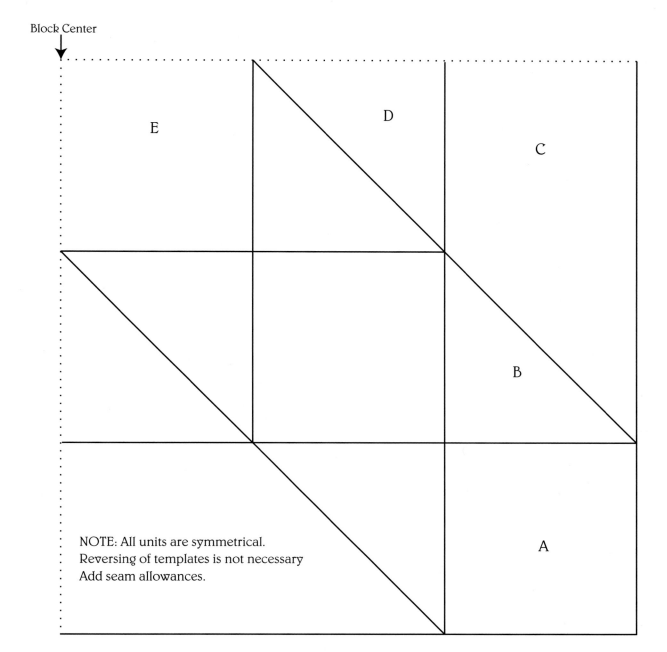

E

D

C

B

A

NOTE: All units are symmetrical.
Reversing of templates is not necessary
Add seam allowances.

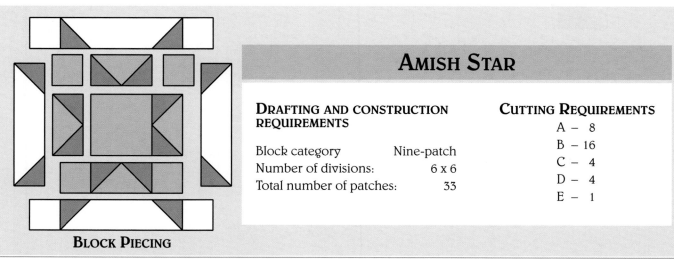

AMISH STAR

DRAFTING AND CONSTRUCTION REQUIREMENTS

Block category	Nine-patch
Number of divisions:	6 x 6
Total number of patches:	33

CUTTING REQUIREMENTS

A – 8
B – 16
C – 4
D – 4
E – 1

BLOCK PIECING

BORDER DESIGN:

DOGTOOTH AND SPLIT SQUARES

For the full-size quilt, a 2" pieced border of triangles is placed between a 2" inner border and a 3" outer border. The border has a total width of 7". For the miniature quilt, halve these dimensions.

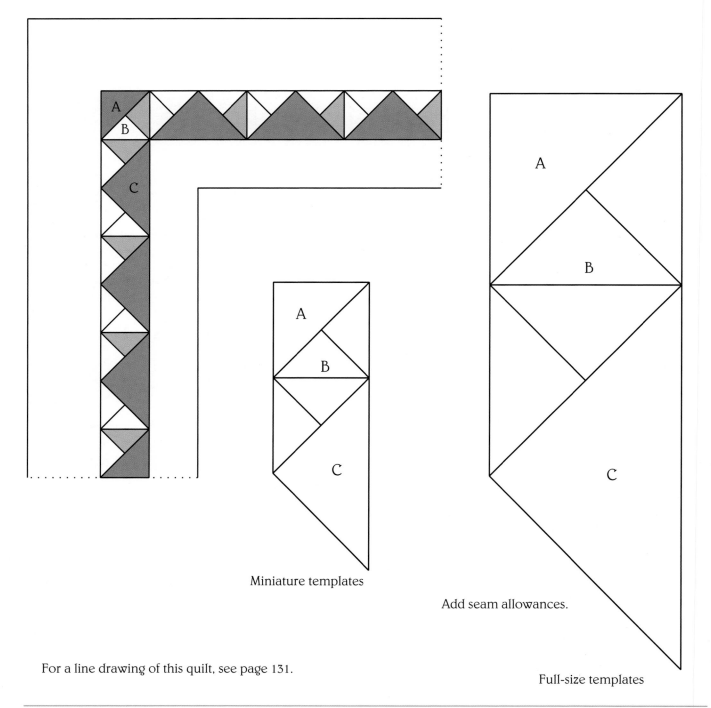

Miniature templates

Add seam allowances.

Full-size templates

For a line drawing of this quilt, see page 131.

WOOD LILY

ARABIAN STAR

DOGTOOTH AND SQUARES BORDER

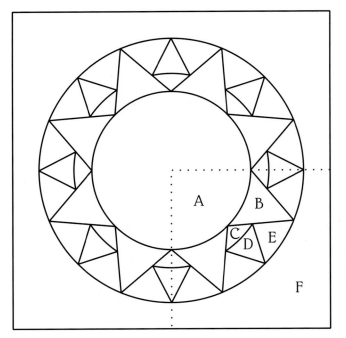

Arabian Star

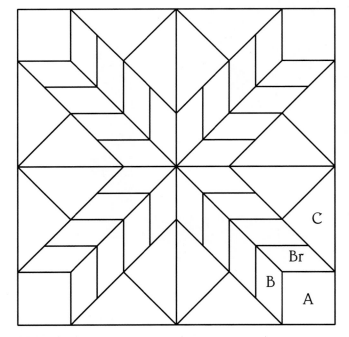

Wood Lily

CIRCLE DESIGN:

ARABIAN STAR

This "stellar or solar variant" is derived from Arabian sources as documented in Clarence P. Hornung's *Handbook of Designs and Devices*. The design contains the basic characteristics of the Mariner's Compasses in Designs 3 and 5. The large center circle provides an opportunity to showcase a large-scale patterned fabric. In the 1920s and 1930s, 32-point versions of this design with a smaller inner circle were published under the name Sunburst. Two outstanding nineteenth century Mariner's Compass quilts use this basic design but have a much smaller inner circle and 64 very narrow points. Both incorporate appliquéd leaf motifs between the compasses. The earliest of these quilts (c. 1830–1840s) is in the Shelburne Museum and the mid-nineteenth century quilt is in the Museum of the City of New York and pictured on page 9. In 1929, the 64-point version of the design was published as Rising Sun.

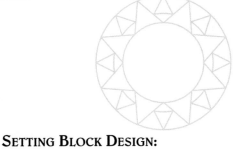

SETTING BLOCK DESIGN:

WOOD LILY

The inspiration for this design is a 1936 *Kansas City Star* pattern that was called Wood Lily or Indian Head. The original design was also published by a *Chicago Tribune* syndicated columnist as St. Elmo's Fire. In the Wood Lily pattern, the division of the split squares runs parallel to the sides of the blocks rather than projecting from the center as it does in this variation.

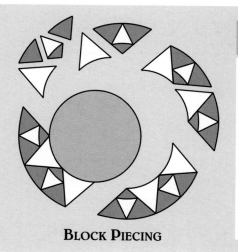

BLOCK PIECING

ARABIAN STAR

DRAFTING AND CONSTRUCTION REQUIREMENTS

Number of points: 16
Number of divisions: 16

RADIUS OF CIRCLES

For 12" block: 3", 5"
For 6" block: 1½", 2½"
Total number of patches: 42

CUTTING REQUIREMENTS

A – 1
B – 8
C – 8
D – 8
E – 16
F – 1

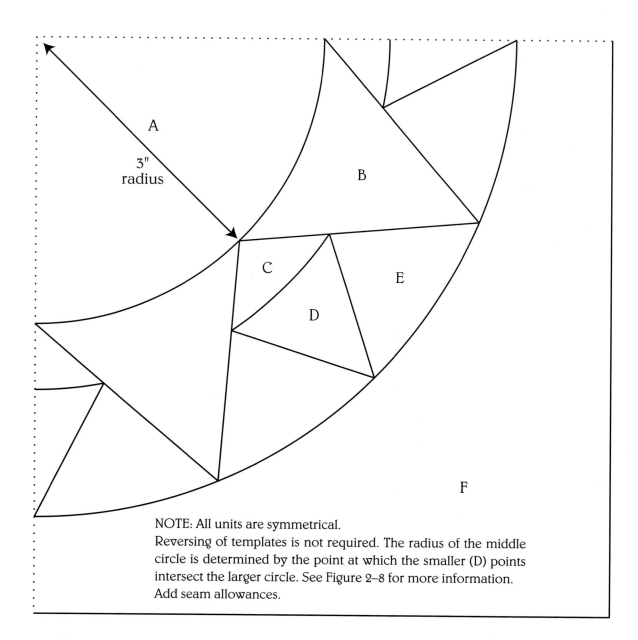

A
3" radius

B

C

E

D

F

NOTE: All units are symmetrical.
Reversing of templates is not required. The radius of the middle circle is determined by the point at which the smaller (D) points intersect the larger circle. See Figure 2–8 for more information.
Add seam allowances.

Block Center

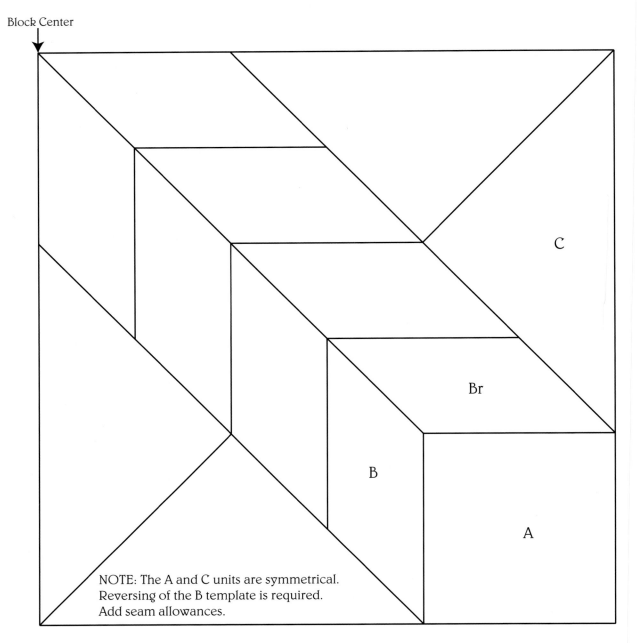

C

Br

B

A

NOTE: The A and C units are symmetrical.
Reversing of the B template is required.
Add seam allowances.

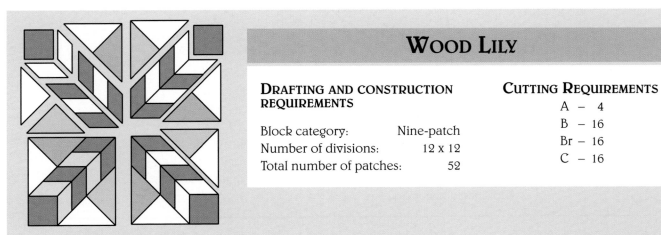

BLOCK PIECING

WOOD LILY

DRAFTING AND CONSTRUCTION REQUIREMENTS

Block category:	Nine-patch
Number of divisions:	12 x 12
Total number of patches:	52

CUTTING REQUIREMENTS

A – 4
B – 16
Br – 16
C – 16

BORDER DESIGN:

DOGTOOTH AND SQUARES

A 2" pieced border is placed between a 2" inner border and a 3" outer border. The border has a total width of 7". These dimensions are for the full-size quilt and are halved for the miniature quilt.

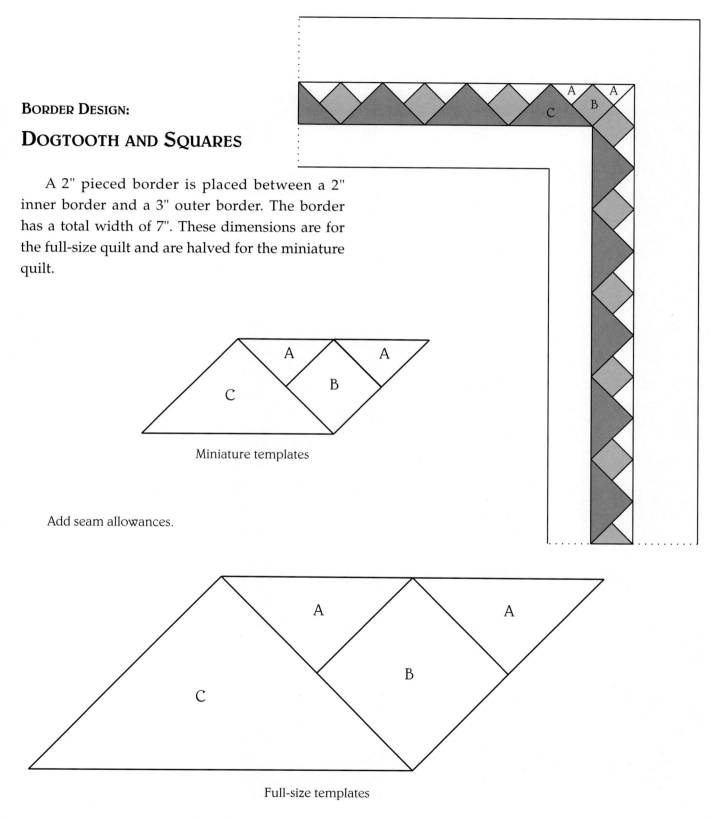

Miniature templates

Add seam allowances.

Full-size templates

For a line drawing of this quilt, see page 132.

DESIGN 8   KANSAS SUNFLOWER & OLD MAID'S RAMBLE

OLD MAID'S RAMBLE

KANSAS SUNFLOWER

DIAMONDS BORDER

CIRCLE DESIGN:

KANSAS SUNFLOWER

This 8-point Kansas Sunflower is among the simplest of the Sunflower designs, which vary from 8 to 25 petals. Carrie Hall included it without comment in her 1935 collection of reproduction quilt blocks. Marguerite Ickis illustrated it in 1949, and recommended appliquéing the diamonds and center to a larger square of patterned fabric. Despite its simplicity, this block is still visually effective. For the 16-petal version, see Design 9.

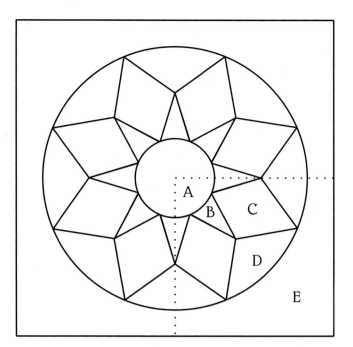

Kansas Sunflower

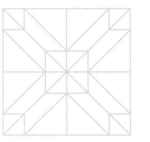

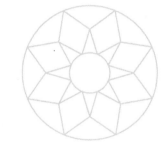

SETTING BLOCK DESIGN:

OLD MAID'S RAMBLE

In 1903, one quarter of this block design was published as Old Maid's Ramble. When four of these smaller blocks rotate around a center point, this striking design is the result. The full block design was also published in the 1930s with the names Feather Bone Block and Gretchen.

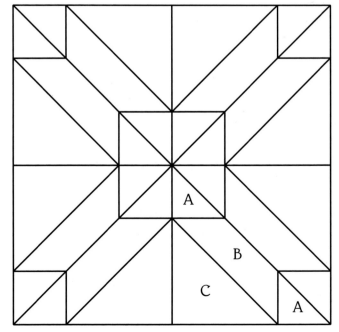

Old Maid's Ramble

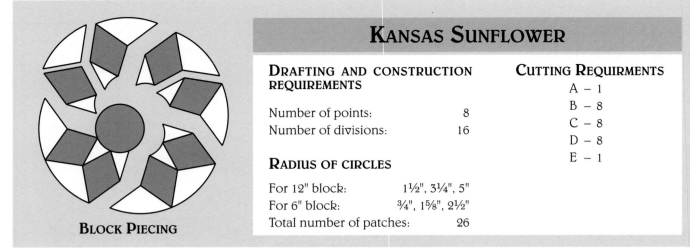

BLOCK PIECING

KANSAS SUNFLOWER

DRAFTING AND CONSTRUCTION REQUIREMENTS

Number of points:	8
Number of divisions:	16

RADIUS OF CIRCLES

For 12" block:	1½", 3¼", 5"
For 6" block:	¾", 1⅝", 2½"
Total number of patches:	26

CUTTING REQUIRMENTS

A – 1
B – 8
C – 8
D – 8
E – 1

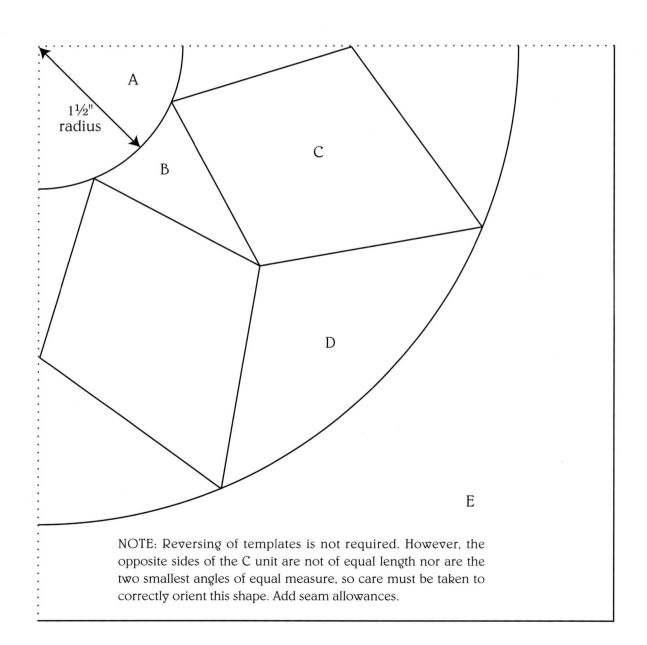

1½" radius

NOTE: Reversing of templates is not required. However, the opposite sides of the C unit are not of equal length nor are the two smallest angles of equal measure, so care must be taken to correctly orient this shape. Add seam allowances.

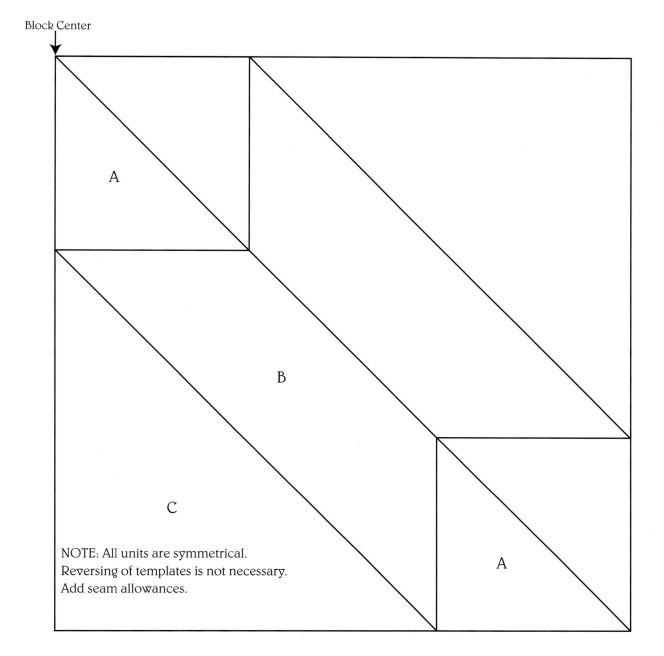

Block Center

A

B

C

A

NOTE: All units are symmetrical.
Reversing of templates is not necessary.
Add seam allowances.

BLOCK PIECING

OLD MAID'S RAMBLE

DRAFTING AND CONSTRUCTION REQUIREMENTS		CUTTING REQUIREMENTS
		A – 16
Block category:	Nine-patch	B – 8
Number of divisions:	6 x 6	C – 8
Total number of patches:	32	

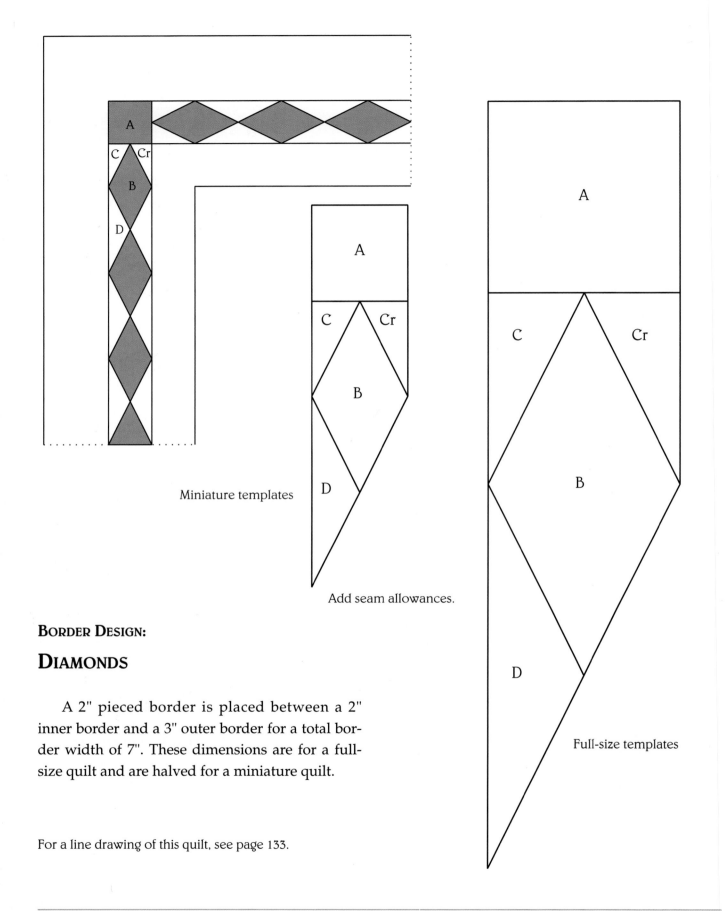

Miniature templates

Add seam allowances.

Full-size templates

BORDER DESIGN:

DIAMONDS

A 2" pieced border is placed between a 2" inner border and a 3" outer border for a total border width of 7". These dimensions are for a full-size quilt and are halved for a miniature quilt.

For a line drawing of this quilt, see page 133.

KANSAS TROUBLES

SUNFLOWER

SAWTOOTH BORDER

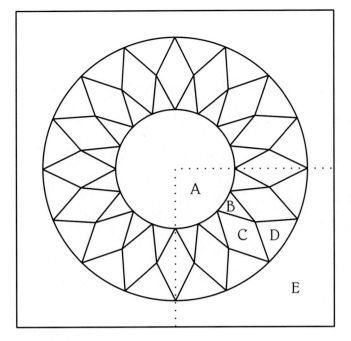

Sunflower

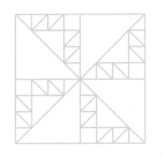

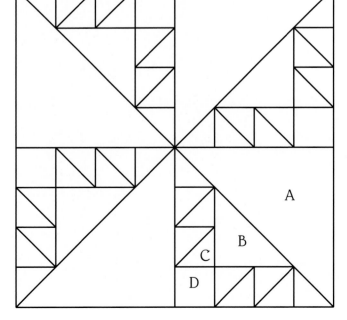

Kansas Troubles

CIRCLE DESIGN:

SUNFLOWER

Sunflower and Sunburst are the names most commonly associated with nineteenth century quilts that utilize this design. It has been suggested that the design originated in Connecticut around 1825. Certainly, it was very popular by mid-century. Sunflower quilts were made by quiltmakers from Canada to Texas and from the East Coast to the Midwest. When the design was published in 1906, it was called Rising Sun. Later publications identified it as Noonday, Kansas Sunflower, Russian Sunflower, Oklahoma Sunburst, and A Brave Sunflower. The last three names were ascribed by the *Kansas City Star* when they offered the design in the 1930s. See Design 8 for an 8-petal version.

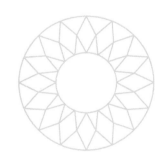

SETTING BLOCK DESIGN:

KANSAS TROUBLES

Kansas Troubles was published by the *Ladies Art Company* in the late 1890s. *Farm Journal* called it Grand Right & Left. This block design can be found with the pinwheels rotating in either direction.

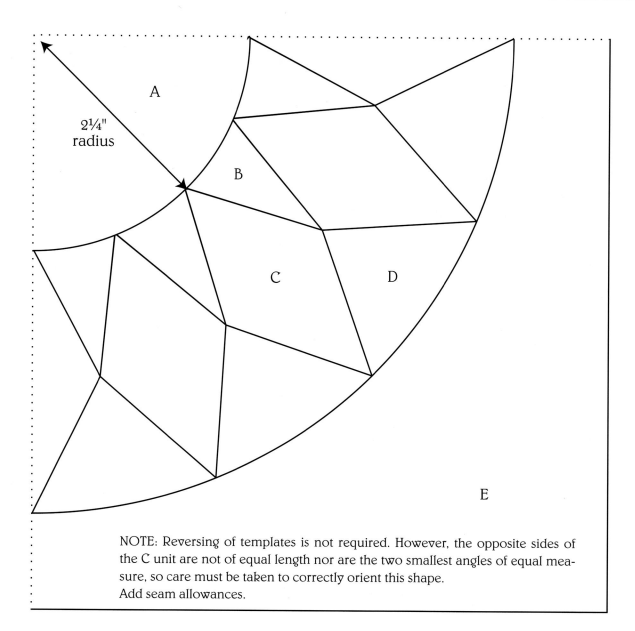

A

2¼"
radius

B

C   D

E

NOTE: Reversing of templates is not required. However, the opposite sides of the C unit are not of equal length nor are the two smallest angles of equal measure, so care must be taken to correctly orient this shape.
Add seam allowances.

BLOCK PIECING

SUNFLOWER

DRAFTING AND CONSTRUCTION REQUIREMENTS

Number of points:	16
Number of divisions:	32

RADIUS OF CIRCLES

For 12" block:	2¼", 3⅝", 5"
For 6" block:	1⅛", 1¹³⁄₁₆", 2½"
Total number of patches:	50

CUTTING REQUIREMENTS

A – 1
B – 16
C – 16
D – 16
E – 1

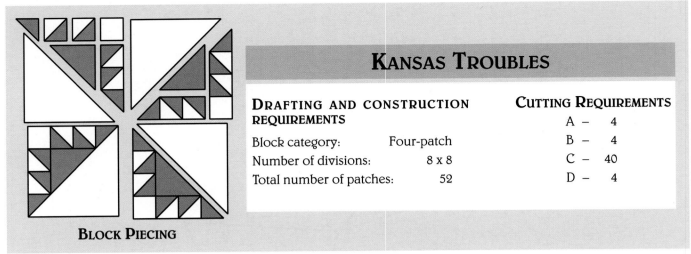

KANSAS TROUBLES

BLOCK PIECING

DRAFTING AND CONSTRUCTION REQUIREMENTS

Block category:	Four-patch
Number of divisions:	8 x 8
Total number of patches:	52

CUTTING REQUIREMENTS

A	–	4
B	–	4
C	–	40
D	–	4

Block Center

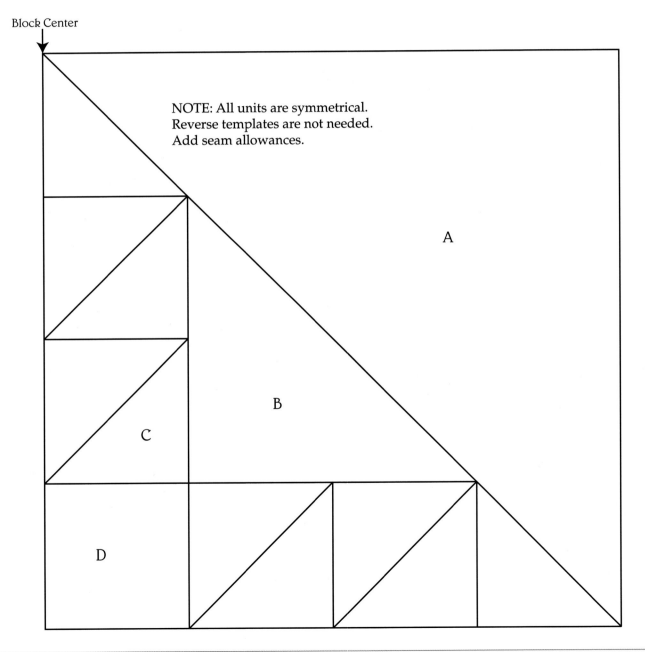

NOTE: All units are symmetrical.
Reverse templates are not needed.
Add seam allowances.

A

B

C

D

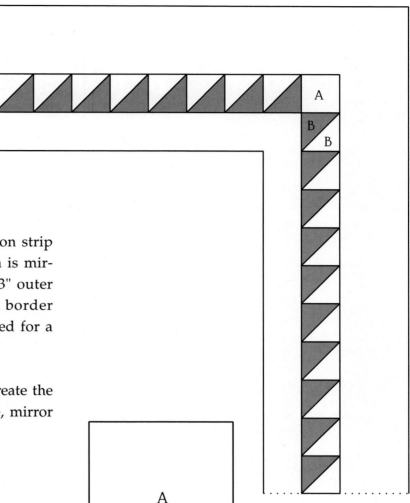

BORDER DESIGN:

SAWTOOTH

For the full-size quilt, a 1½" transition strip precedes a 1½" Sawtooth border, which is mirrored at the center of all four sides. A 3" outer border completes the quilt for a total border width of 6". These dimensions are halved for a miniature quilt.

NOTE: This border is mirrored. To create the larger triangle at the center of each side, mirror unit B along one short side.

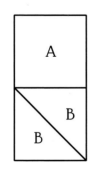

Miniature templates

Add seam allowances.

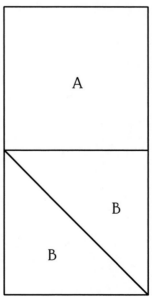

Full-size templates

For a line drawing of this quilt, see page 134.

MARIGOLD & AUNTIE'S FAVORITE©

AUNTIE'S FAVORITE©

MARIGOLD

CHECKERBOARD BORDER

CIRCLE DESIGN:

MARIGOLD

An 1850 quilt by Mrs. Castro Jane Harris Moore of Folsum, Alabama, is the source of this colorful quilt name. The quilt is illustrated in Mary Elizabeth Johnson's *A Garden of Quilts*. Johnson states that the name comes from "Mary's Gold" and refers to the Virgin Mary. The yellow marigolds in the 1850 quilt are surrounded by red triangles, placed on white background squares, and set together with teal sashing. Although this design is also called Sunflower, the large center circle and small petals differentiate it from other blocks with the same name. The large circle also offers an opportunity to feature a large-scale patterned fabric.

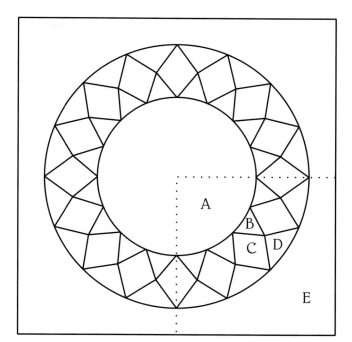

Marigold

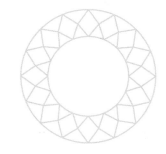

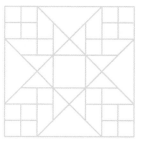

SETTING BLOCK DESIGN:

AUNTIE'S FAVORITE©

Auntie's Favorite© is from Judy Martin's, *The Block Book* (used with permission). It contains elements of traditional blocks, such as the Ohio Star in the center and Four-patch blocks in the corners.

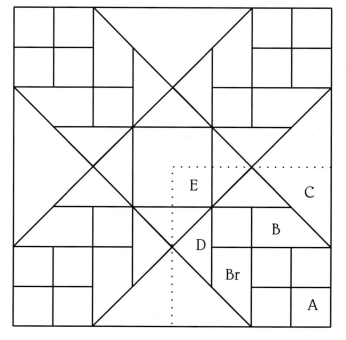

Auntie's Favorite©

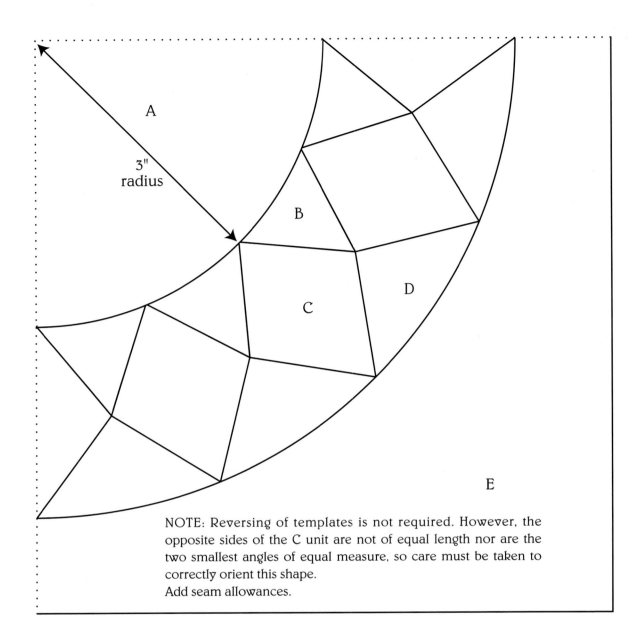

A

3"
radius

B

C

D

E

NOTE: Reversing of templates is not required. However, the opposite sides of the C unit are not of equal length nor are the two smallest angles of equal measure, so care must be taken to correctly orient this shape.
Add seam allowances.

MARIGOLD

BLOCK PIECING

DRAFTING AND CONSTRUCTION REQUIREMENTS

Number of points:	16
Number of divisions:	32

RADIUS OF CIRCLES

For 12" block:	3", 4", 5"
For 6" block:	1½", 2", 2½"
Total number of patches:	50

CUTTING REQUIREMENTS

A – 1
B – 16
C – 16
D – 16
E – 1

BLOCK PIECING

AUNTIE'S FAVORITE©

DRAFTING AND CONSTRUCTION REQUIREMENTS

Block Category:	Four-patch
Number of divisions:	8 x 8
Total number of patches:	45

CUTTING REQUIREMENTS

A – 20
B – 4
Br – 4
C – 4
D – 12
E – 1

Block Center

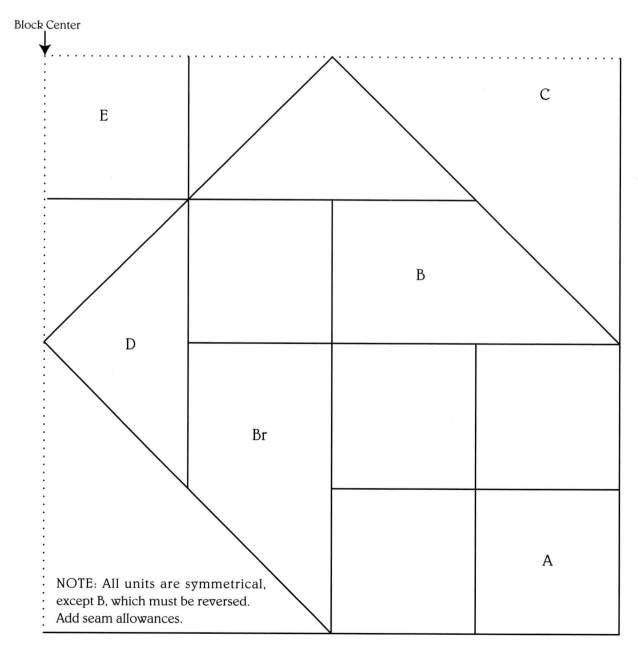

NOTE: All units are symmetrical, except B, which must be reversed. Add seam allowances.

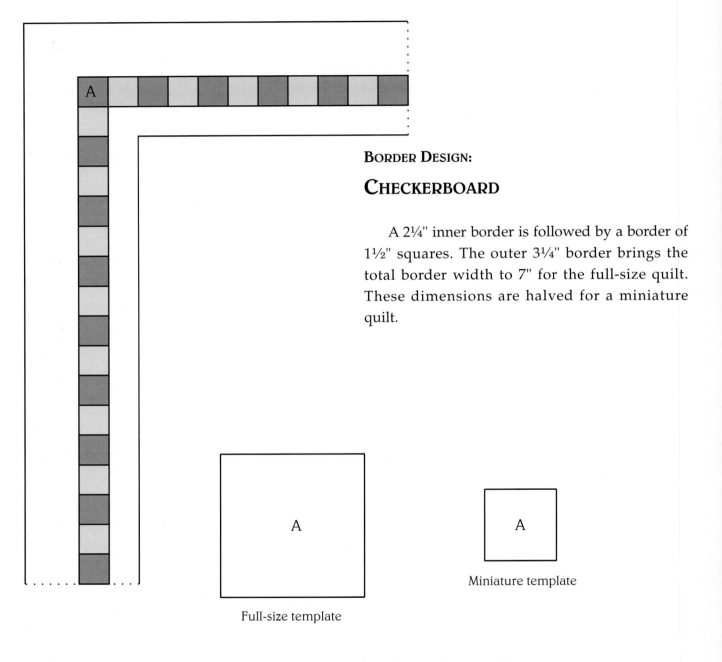

Border Design:

Checkerboard

A 2¼" inner border is followed by a border of 1½" squares. The outer 3¼" border brings the total border width to 7" for the full-size quilt. These dimensions are halved for a miniature quilt.

Full-size template

Miniature template

Add seam allowances.

For a line drawing of this quilt, see page 135.

DESIGN 11

COUNTRY ROADS

SUNFLOWER

TRIANGLES BORDER

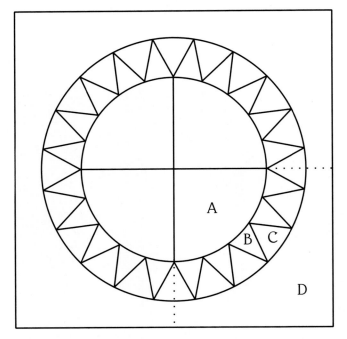

Sunflower

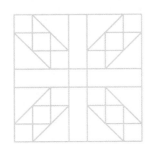

CIRCLE DESIGN:

SUNFLOWER

A late nineteenth-century scrap quilt by Betty Quackenbush of North Carolina is the source for this Sunflower block. While this pattern has not been published in this exact form, a 1929 design called Indian Summer has the same basic characteristics. However, its four fan-like shapes are arranged so the four quarter circles are at the corners rather than the center. When set block-to-block, an overall Sunflower design is achieved. In 1932, a single quadrant of the design was offered by a syndicated *Chicago Tribune* columnist under the name Chinese Fan. Four rotated Chinese Fan blocks also result in this design. An alternative to the pieced center is a single large circle. Called a Sunburst, this variation is found in both nineteenth and twentieth century quilts, although the number of points varies.

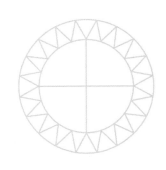

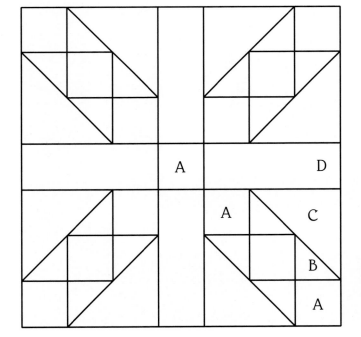

Country Roads

SETTING BLOCK DESIGN:

COUNTRY ROADS

Country Roads is a relatively recent name for this design. By the 1930s, the design had been published under the names Buffalo Ridge and Grandmother's Fancy. Seven-patch block designs make up a relatively small percentage of all designs, which adds to Country Roads' appeal.

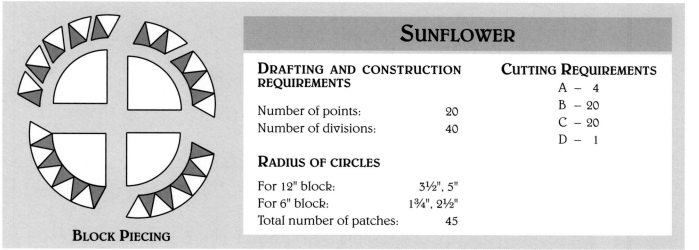

SUNFLOWER

BLOCK PIECING

DRAFTING AND CONSTRUCTION REQUIREMENTS

Number of points: 20
Number of divisions: 40

RADIUS OF CIRCLES

For 12" block: 3½", 5"
For 6" block: 1¾", 2½"
Total number of patches: 45

CUTTING REQUIREMENTS

A – 4
B – 20
C – 20
D – 1

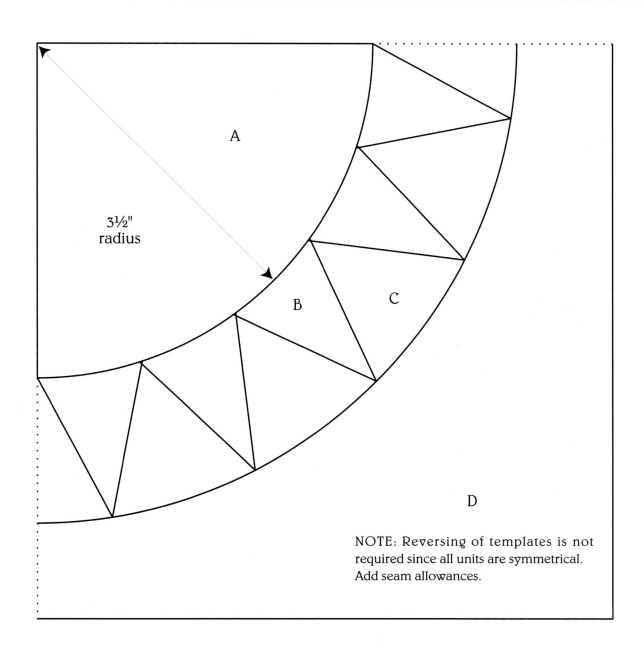

A

3½"
radius

B

C

D

NOTE: Reversing of templates is not
required since all units are symmetrical.
Add seam allowances.

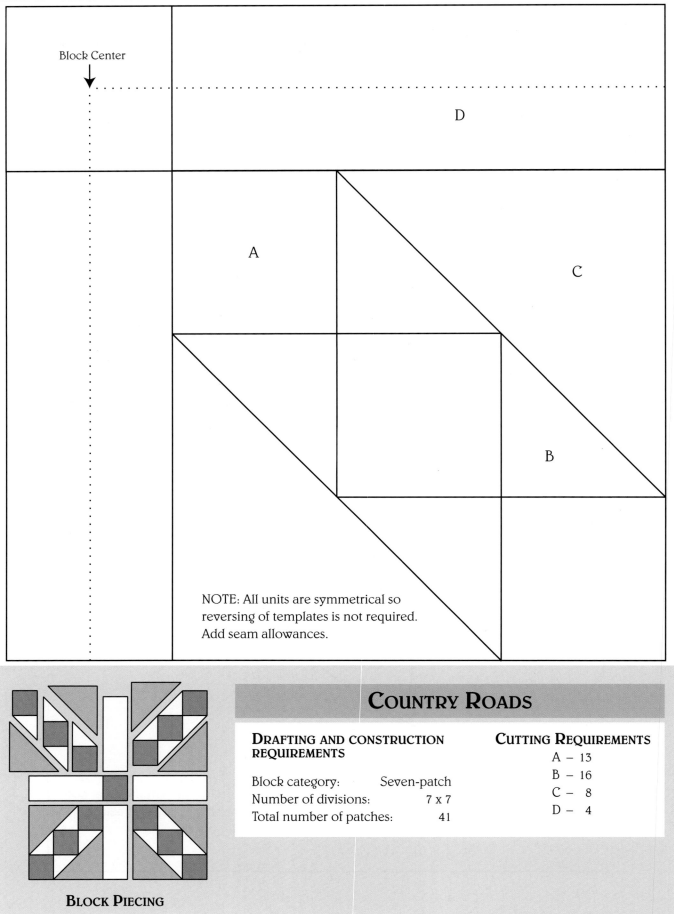

Block Center

D

A

C

B

NOTE: All units are symmetrical so reversing of templates is not required. Add seam allowances.

COUNTRY ROADS

DRAFTING AND CONSTRUCTION REQUIREMENTS

Block category: Seven-patch
Number of divisions: 7 x 7
Total number of patches: 41

CUTTING REQUIREMENTS

A – 13
B – 16
C – 8
D – 4

BLOCK PIECING

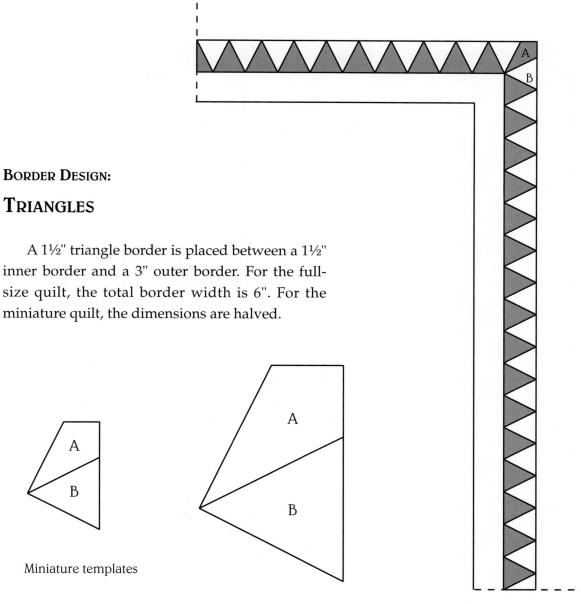

BORDER DESIGN:

TRIANGLES

A 1½" triangle border is placed between a 1½" inner border and a 3" outer border. For the full-size quilt, the total border width is 6". For the miniature quilt, the dimensions are halved.

Miniature templates

Full-size templates

Add seam allowances.

For a line drawing of this quilt, see page 136.

DESIGN 12

WYOMING VALLEY

SINGLE SUNFLOWER

DOGTOOTH BORDER

CIRCLE DESIGN:

SINGLE SUNFLOWER

This 12-point Single Sunflower block is a variation of the 16-point design that was offered by the *Ladies Art Company* in the 1890s. In 1935, Carrie Hall illustrated the 16-point design, calling it Sunflower but also mentioned it was known as Blazing Sun or Blazing Star.

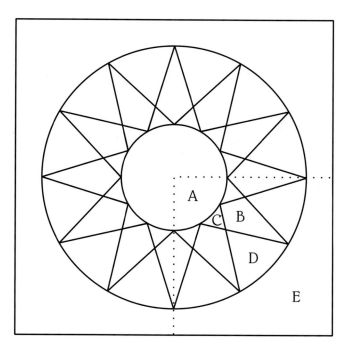

Single Sunflower

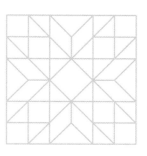

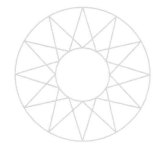

SETTING BLOCK DESIGN:

WYOMING VALLEY

This is a slight variation of the Wyoming Valley block, which was published by a *Chicago Tribune* syndicated columnist in the 1930s. It has also appeared in recent publications that are associated with *Quilter's Newsletter Magazine*.

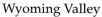

Wyoming Valley

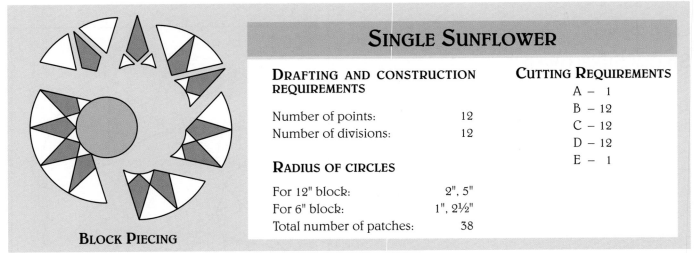

BLOCK PIECING

SINGLE SUNFLOWER

DRAFTING AND CONSTRUCTION REQUIREMENTS

Number of points: 12
Number of divisions: 12

RADIUS OF CIRCLES

For 12" block: 2", 5"
For 6" block: 1", 2½"
Total number of patches: 38

CUTTING REQUIREMENTS

A – 1
B – 12
C – 12
D – 12
E – 1

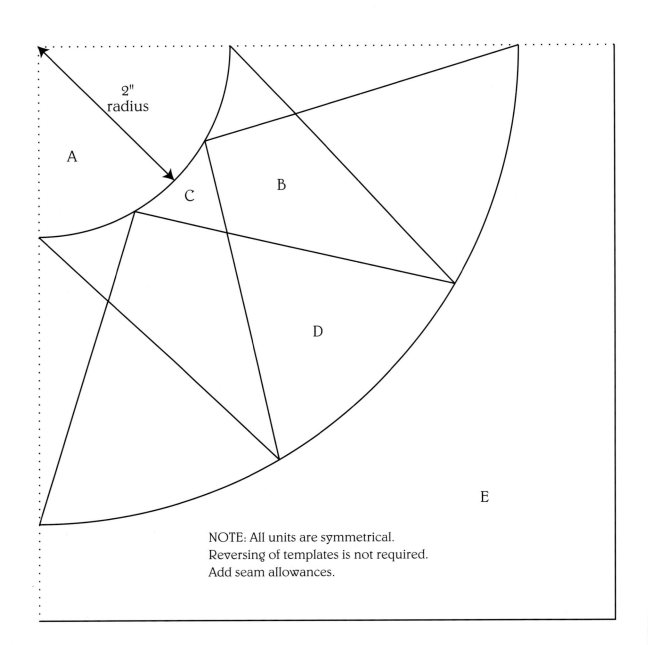

2"
radius

A

C

B

D

E

NOTE: All units are symmetrical.
Reversing of templates is not required.
Add seam allowances.

Block Center

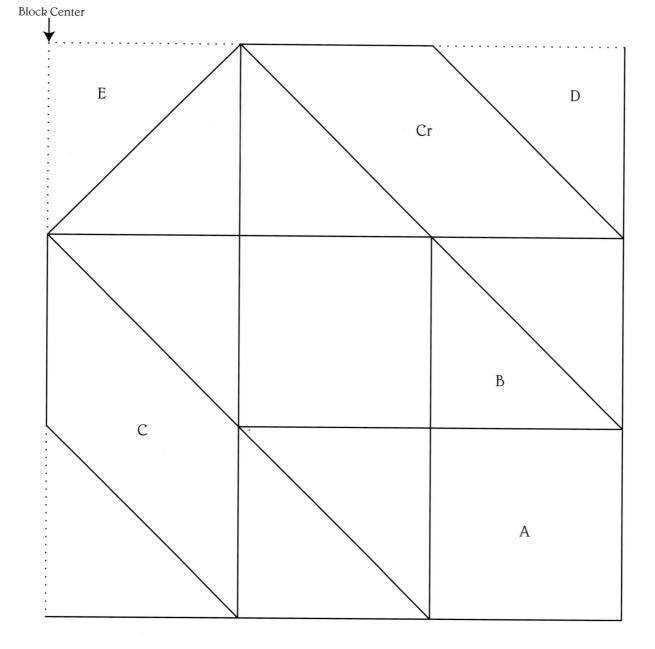

E

Cr

D

B

C

A

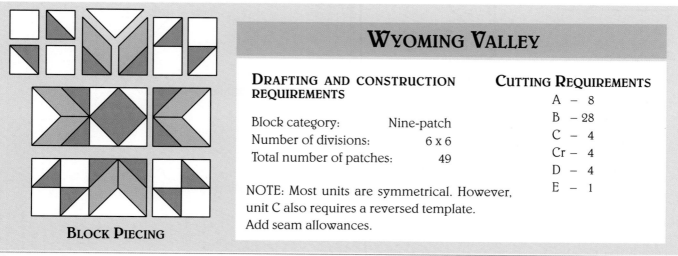

BLOCK PIECING

WYOMING VALLEY

DRAFTING AND CONSTRUCTION REQUIREMENTS		CUTTING REQUIREMENTS
Block category:	Nine-patch	A – 8
Number of divisions:	6 x 6	B – 28
Total number of patches:	49	C – 4
		Cr – 4
		D – 4
		E – 1

NOTE: Most units are symmetrical. However, unit C also requires a reversed template. Add seam allowances.

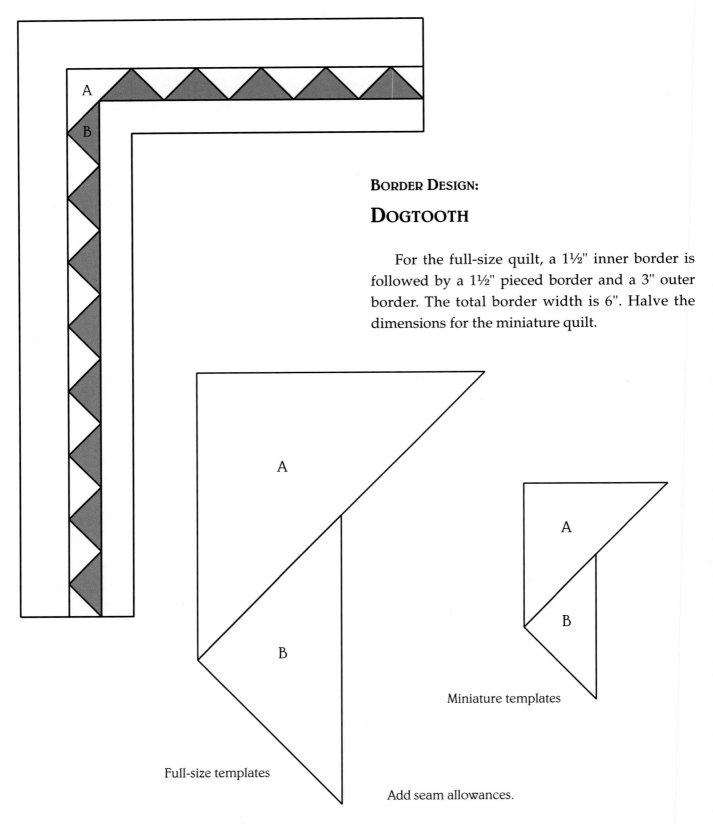

Border Design:

Dogtooth

For the full-size quilt, a 1½" inner border is followed by a 1½" pieced border and a 3" outer border. The total border width is 6". Halve the dimensions for the miniature quilt.

Miniature templates

Full-size templates

Add seam allowances.

For a line drawing of this quilt, see page 137.

DESIGN 13

JOSEPH'S
COAT

WHEEL OF
FORTUNE

BROKEN
DISHES
BORDER

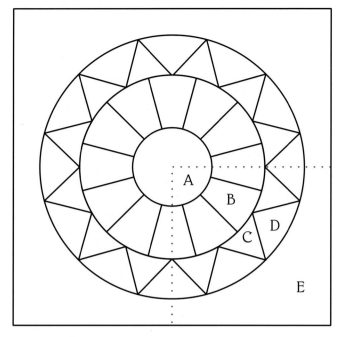

Wheel of Fortune

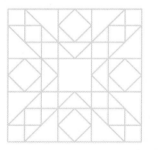

CIRCLE DESIGN:

WHEEL OF FORTUNE

The original Wheel of Fortune design was not set into a circle. Rather, lines were drawn from the tips of the triangular points to the edge of the square, creating background units of triangles and irregular pentagons. Wheel of Fortune was one of many quilt patterns offered for decades to newspaper readers through mail order distributors such as the Old Chelsea Station Needlecraft Service. Text accompanying the pattern consistently recommended the use of colorful scraps.

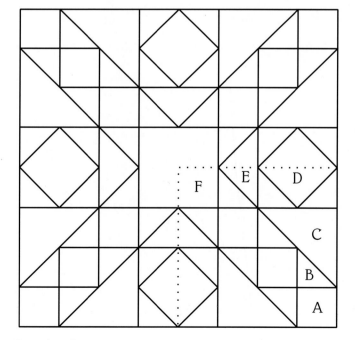

Joseph's Coat

SETTING BLOCK DESIGN:

JOSEPH'S COAT

Ladies Art Company published Joseph's Coat in the 1890s. It was also called Lewis and Clark in a 1906 booklet of quilt patterns. In 1935, Carrie Hall illustrated Joseph's Coat noting that it was ideal for using scraps, and even called Scrapbag in Pennsylvania. The block was also published as Mrs. Thomas in a syndicated mail-order column that appeared in the second quarter of the twentieth century.

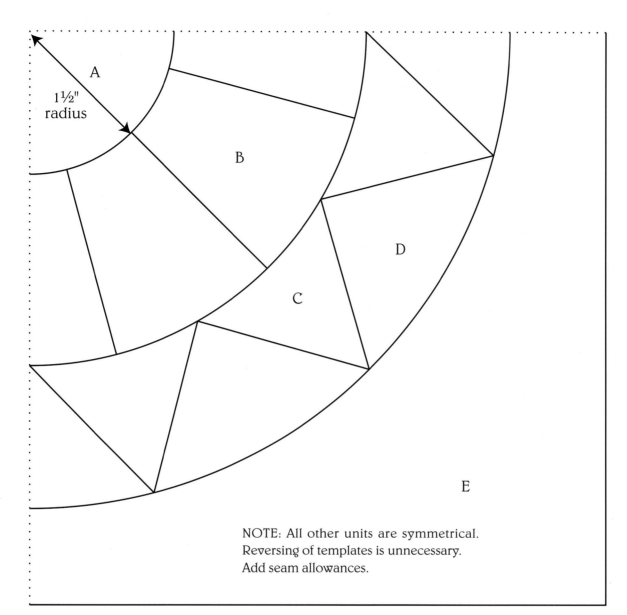

1½"
radius

A

B

C

D

E

NOTE: All other units are symmetrical.
Reversing of templates is unnecessary.
Add seam allowances.

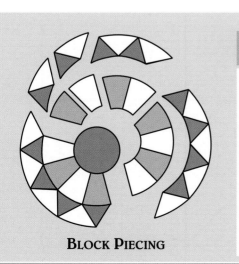

BLOCK PIECING

WHEEL OF FORTUNE

DRAFTING AND CONSTRUCTION REQUIREMENTS

Number of points:	12
Number of divisions:	24

RADIUS OF CIRCLES

For 12" block:	1½", 3½", 5"
For 6" block:	¾", 1¾", 2½"
Total number of patches:	38

CUTTING REQUIREMENTS

A – 1
B – 12
C – 12
D – 12
E – 1

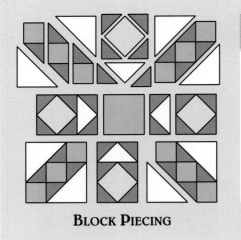

BLOCK PIECING

JOSEPH'S COAT

DRAFTING AND CONSTRUCTION REQUIREMENTS

Block category:	Four-patch
Number of divisions:	8 x 8
Total number of patches:	69

CUTTING REQUIREMENTS

A – 12
B – 40
C – 8
D – 4
E – 4
F – 1

Block Center

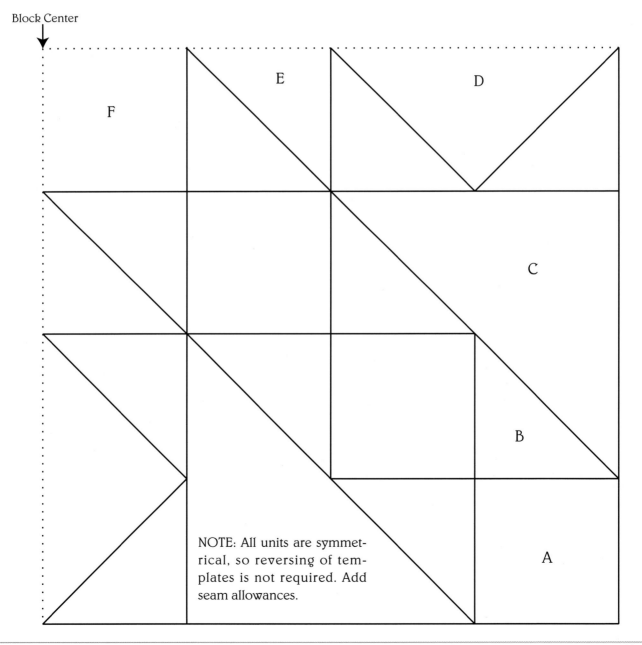

F

E

D

C

B

A

NOTE: All units are symmetrical, so reversing of templates is not required. Add seam allowances.

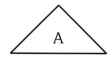

BORDER DESIGN:

BROKEN DISHES

For the full-size quilt, a 2" pieced border is surrounded by a 2" inner border and a 3" outer border. The result is a total border width of 7". For the miniature quilt, halve these dimensions.

A

Full-size template

A

Miniature template

Add seam allowances.

For a line drawing of this quilt, see page 138.

DESIGN 14   FEATHERED STAR & SHADED CROSSROAD©

SHADED CROSSROAD©

FEATHERED STAR

SURROUNDED SQUARES BORDER

CIRCLE DESIGN:

FEATHERED STAR

Feathered Star was advertised in newspapers and made available to readers by mail order from Old Chelsea Station Needlecraft Service, which began in the 1930s. While it was illustrated as a scrap quilt, the text also indicated that it could be made with a more limited number of fabrics.

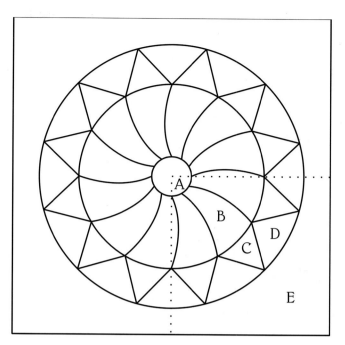

Feathered Star

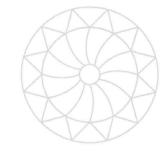

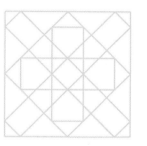

SETTING BLOCK DESIGN:

SHADED CROSSROAD©

Shaded Crossroad© appears to be a relatively recent design that has both + and x designs, surrounded by square shapes. It can be found in Maggie Malone's *500 Full-Size Patchwork Patterns* (used with permission).

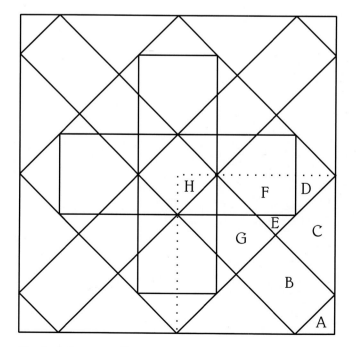

Shaded Crossroad©

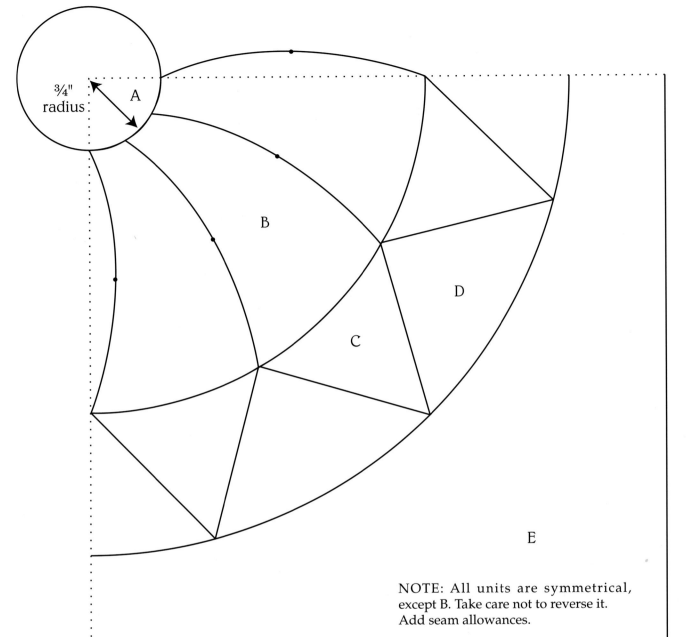

¾"
radius

A

B

C

D

E

NOTE: All units are symmetrical, except B. Take care not to reverse it. Add seam allowances.

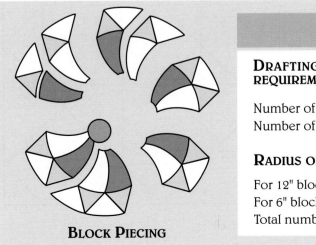

BLOCK PIECING

FEATHERED STAR

DRAFTING AND CONSTRUCTION REQUIREMENTS

Number of points:	12
Number of divisions:	24

RADIUS OF CIRCLES

For 12" block:	¾", 3½", 5"
For 6" block:	⅜", 1¾", 2½"
Total number of patches:	38

CUTTING REQUIREMENTS

A – 1
B – 12
C – 12
D – 12
E – 1

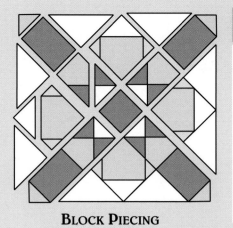

BLOCK PIECING

SHADED CROSSROAD©

DRAFTING AND CONSTRUCTION REQUIREMENTS

Block category	Four-patch
Number of divisions:	8 x 8
Total number of patches:	49

CUTTING REQUIREMENTS

A – 16
B – 4
C – 8
D – 4
E – 8
F – 4
G – 4
H – 1

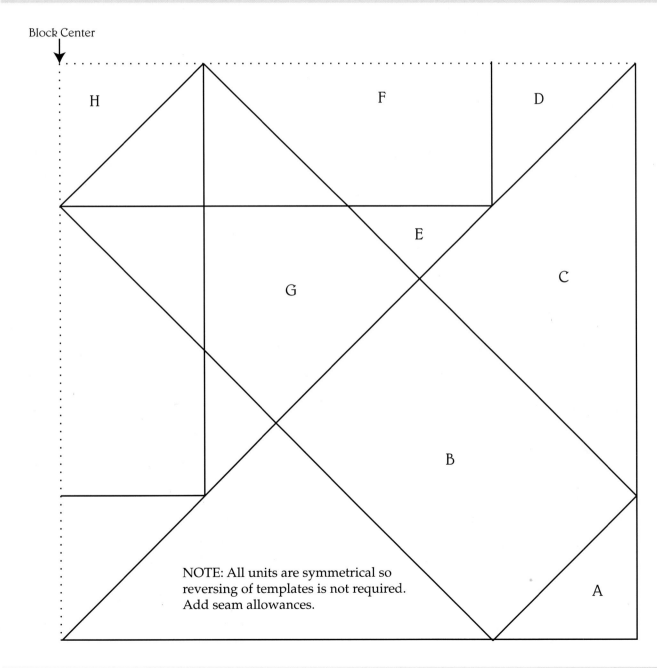

Block Center

H

F

D

E

C

G

B

A

NOTE: All units are symmetrical so reversing of templates is not required. Add seam allowances.

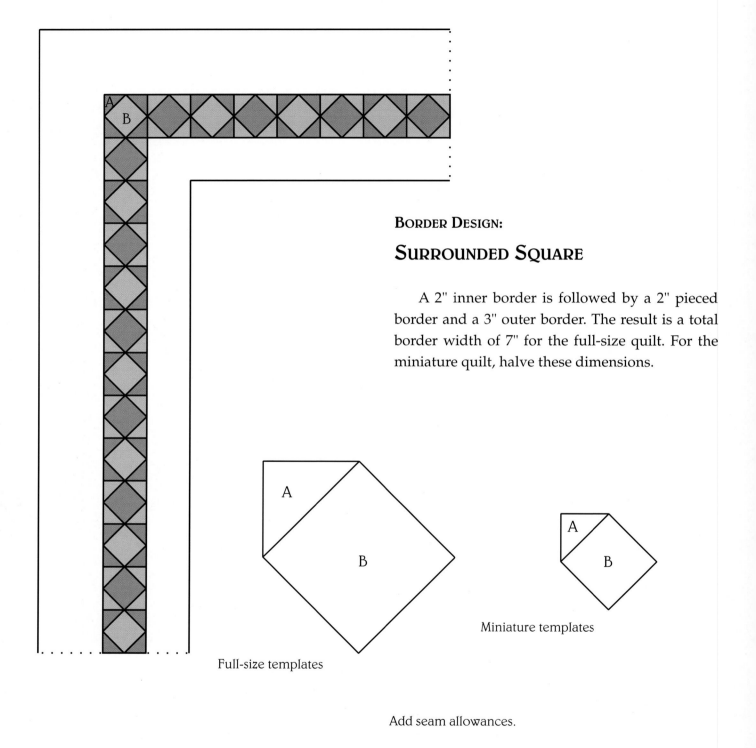

BORDER DESIGN:

SURROUNDED SQUARE

A 2" inner border is followed by a 2" pieced border and a 3" outer border. The result is a total border width of 7" for the full-size quilt. For the miniature quilt, halve these dimensions.

Miniature templates

Full-size templates

Add seam allowances.

For a line drawing of this quilt, see page 139.

WILD GOOSE CHASE

RISING SUN

BIRDS IN FLIGHT BORDER

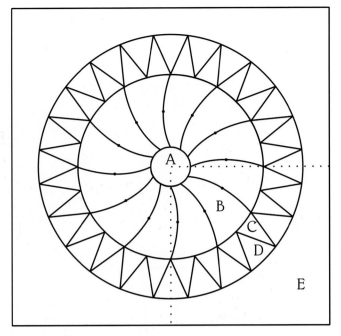

Rising Sun

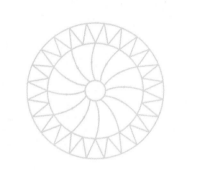

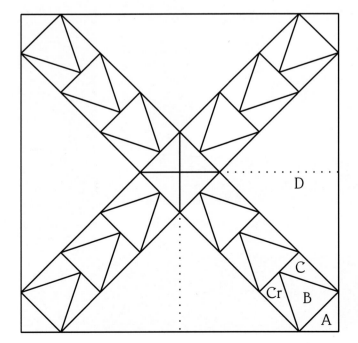

Wild Goose Chase

CIRCLE DESIGN:

RISING SUN

Rising Sun was published by the *Ladies Art Company* in the 1890s. In the 1930s, it appeared in pattern collections by Ruby McKim, Carrie Hall, and others. McKim described the design as intricate "but not enough so to daunt the quilt maker who aspires to a design that is both lovely and unusual." She recommended using flame red and orange for the sun and a white, unbleached muslin, or yellow background for a "stunning counterpane." Rising Sun also appeared in newspapers in the 1930s, including a syndicated *Chicago Tribune* column. The *Kansas City Star* called it Circle Saw and *Hearth and Home* named it Wagon Wheel and Wheel of Fortune, depending on the direction of the blade rotation. Home Art Studios, a mail order pattern service operating in the 1930s, called it Wheel of Life. Additional names for the pattern are Fly Wheel and Cog Wheel.

SETTING BLOCK DESIGN:

WILD GOOSE CHASE

This block was called Odd Fellow's Cross in Maggie Malone's *1001 Patchwork Designs*. However, its design source seems more closely related to Wild Goose Chase, which was published in the 1930's by Ruby McKim and others. (The original Odd Fellows design is the inspiration for the setting block in Design 16.)

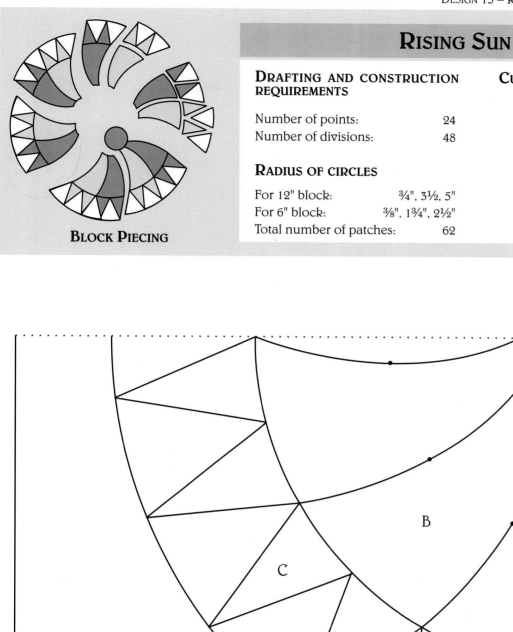

BLOCK PIECING

RISING SUN

DRAFTING AND CONSTRUCTION REQUIREMENTS

Number of points:	24
Number of divisions:	48

RADIUS OF CIRCLES

For 12" block:	¾", 3½, 5"
For 6" block:	⅜", 1¾", 2½"
Total number of patches:	62

CUTTING REQUIREMENTS

A –	1
B –	12
C –	24
D –	24
E –	1

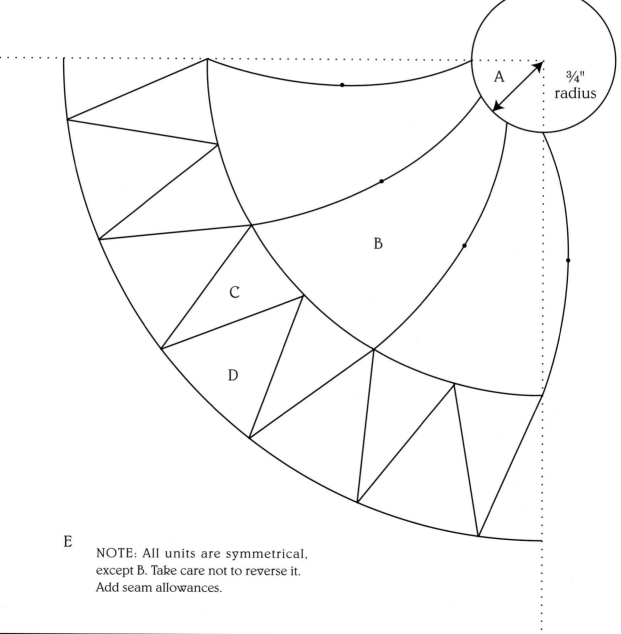

¾"
radius

NOTE: All units are symmetrical, except B. Take care not to reverse it. Add seam allowances.

Block Center

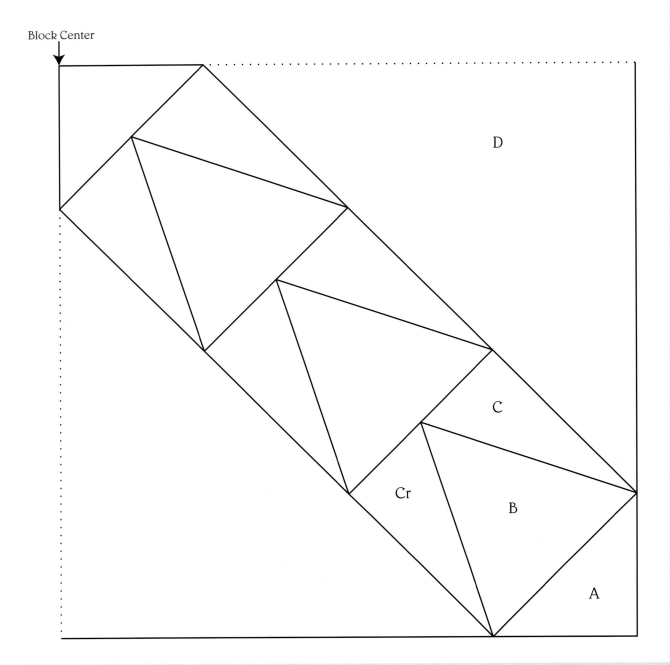

D

C

Cr

B

A

WILD GOOSE CHASE

DRAFTING AND CONSTRUCTION REQUIREMENTS

Block category:	Four-patch
Number of divisions:	8 x 8
Total number of patches:	48

CUTTING REQUIREMENTS

A – 8
B – 12
C – 12
Cr – 12
D – 4

NOTE: All units are symmetrical except C, which requires reversal of half the units.

BLOCK PIECING

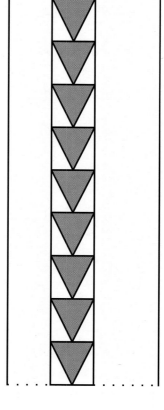

BORDER DESIGN:

BIRDS IN FLIGHT

For a full-size quilt, a 2" inner border precedes a 2" pieced border, which is mirrored at the center of each side. The outer border is 3" wide and the total border width is 7". Halve these dimensions for the miniature quilt.

NOTE: This border is mirrored. To create the larger triangle at the center of each side, mirror the C or Cr unit along the shortest edge.

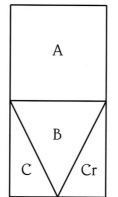

Miniature templates

Add seam allowances.

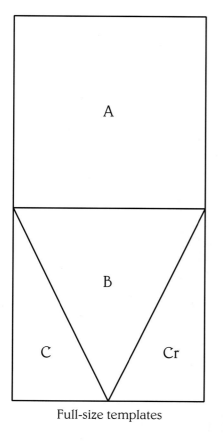

Full-size templates

For a line drawing of this quilt, see page 140.

ODD FELLOWS

SUNBIRDS

FLYING GEESE BORDER

CIRCLE DESIGN:

SUNBIRDS

Sunbirds was inspired by a motif created for the Leading Part Company of Osaka, Japan. It appears in Hajime Ouchi's 1973 publication, *Japanese Optical and Geometrical Art*. I have given it the name Sunbirds.

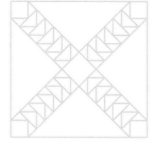

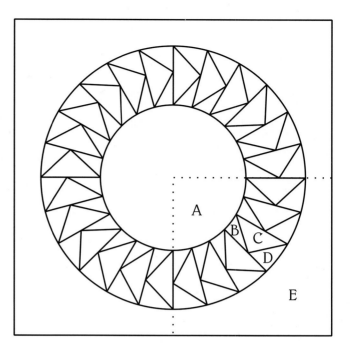

Sunbirds

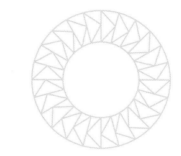

SETTING BLOCK DESIGN:

ODD FELLOWS

In the 1890s, *Ladies Art Company* published the Odd Fellows design that is the basis for this block. The original was a 64-square four-patch and had only two Flying Geese units on each diagonal. This design was published in numerous books, magazines, and newspapers during the 1920s and 1930s under the following names: Flying Geese, Odd Fellows Cross, Odd Fellow's Patch, Baltimore Belle, and An Effective Square. A 16-square four-patch version was published in 1929 as Odd Fellow's Cross. In 1933, the *Kansas City Star* called it Ozark Trails.

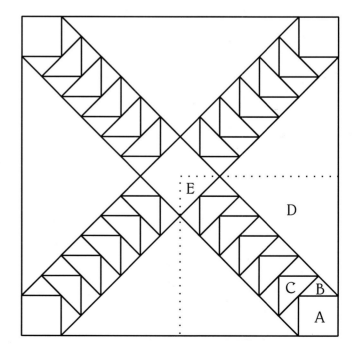

Odd Fellows

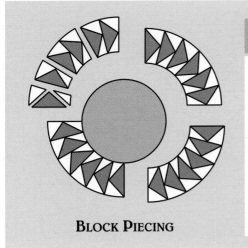

BLOCK PIECING

SUNBIRDS

DRAFTING AND CONSTRUCTION REQUIREMENTS

Number of points:	24
Number of divisions:	24

RADIUS OF CIRCLES

For 12" block:	2¾", 4", 5"
For 6" block:	1⅜", 2", 2½"
Total number of patches:	74

CUTTING REQUIREMENTS

A – 1
B – 24
C – 24
D – 24
E – 1

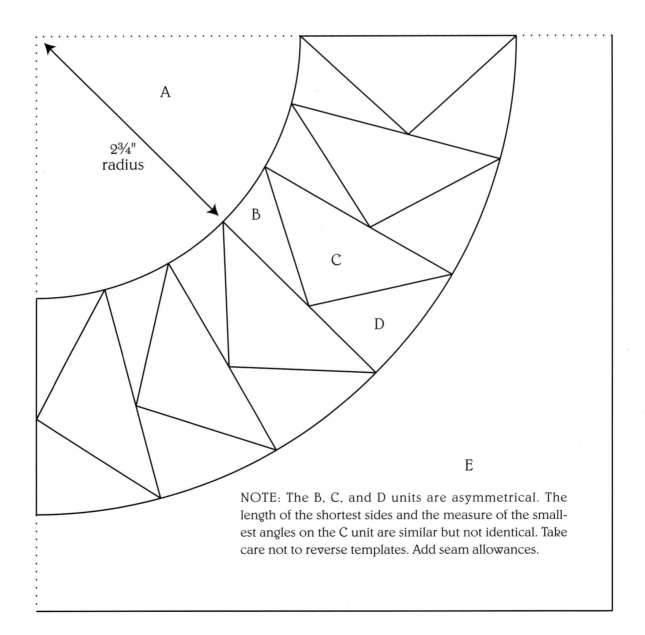

2¾" radius

NOTE: The B, C, and D units are asymmetrical. The length of the shortest sides and the measure of the smallest angles on the C unit are similar but not identical. Take care not to reverse templates. Add seam allowances.

Block Center

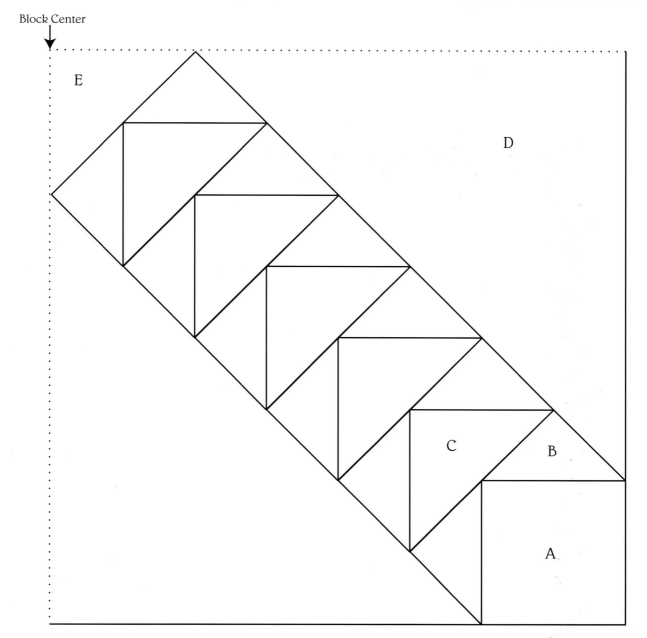

E

D

C

B

A

ODD FELLOWS

DRAFTING AND CONSTRUCTION REQUIREMENTS

Block category: Four-patch
Number of divisions: 16 x 16
Total number of patches: 77

NOTE: All units are symmetrical.
Reversal of templates is not required.
Add seam allowances.

CUTTING REQUIREMENTS

A – 4
B – 48
C – 20
D – 4
E – 1

BLOCK PIECING

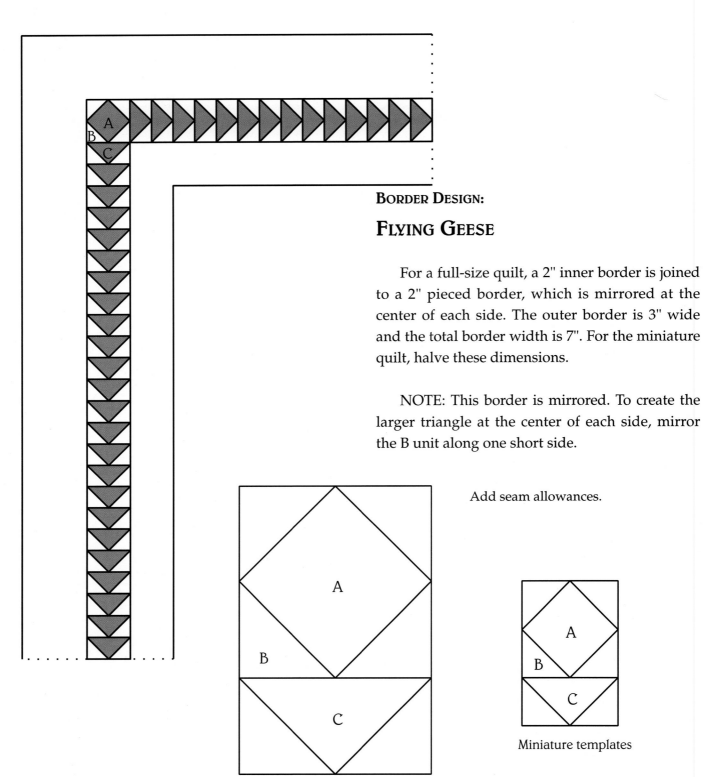

BORDER DESIGN:

FLYING GEESE

For a full-size quilt, a 2" inner border is joined to a 2" pieced border, which is mirrored at the center of each side. The outer border is 3" wide and the total border width is 7". For the miniature quilt, halve these dimensions.

NOTE: This border is mirrored. To create the larger triangle at the center of each side, mirror the B unit along one short side.

Add seam allowances.

Full-size templates

Miniature templates

For a line drawing of this quilt, see page 141.

CHAPTER

5

VARIATIONS

The drawings on pages 118 – 120 are a start on creating variations of the initial quilts. Each variation combines a circular block with a different setting block and a different border design. For example, the first variation uses the Design 5 Sunburst circular block, the Design 16 Odd Fellows setting block, and the Elongated Dogtooth border from Design 1. These variations also show the impact of placing the setting blocks rather than the circular blocks in the corners, as shown in the original designs. This subtle change impacts the overall appearance of the quilts. The six variations only begin to show the flexibility of the interchangeable blocks, sets, and borders, and the variety of quilts that can be created.

As you develop your own quilts, remember to select blocks that share a visual relationship between the sizes and shapes of the patches.

Changing the overall quilt size also needs to be addressed. The line drawings on pages 126 – 141 show 35 blocks, arranged in 5 columns and 7 rows. Using an odd number of blocks is necessary to maintain the symmetry of the design. For the 12" blocks, the quilts measure 72"-78" wide and 84"-88" long, depending on the width of the borders, which range from 6" to 8". For the miniature quilts, the dimensions are 36"-38" wide and 42"-44" long. To change a quilt's dimensions, resist the urge to significantly change the size of the border, as it has been designed to be proportional

with the remainder of the quilt. Instead, the blocks and border may be re-drafted to a larger or smaller size, as discussed in Chapter 2. Or, the number of blocks may be changed. If two columns and/or rows are added or subtracted vertically and/or horizontally, the total number of columns and rows remains odd, and the quilt is still symmetrical. The quilt can be three columns and five rows, or five columns and five rows, or seven columns and seven rows, and so on. If only one column or row is added or subtracted to the width or length, the total number of columns or rows becomes even, and the body of the quilt becomes asymmetrical. That is, two corners have circular blocks and two have setting blocks. This result looks visually unbalanced. The alternative to adding or subtracting a whole column and/or row from one side is to add or subtract a half column and/or row on two opposite sides, thereby maintaining the symmetry of the design.

In the last two line drawings in this chapter, Design 1A, page 121, is shown first with a whole column subtracted from the width and a whole row subtracted from the length. Then, Design 1B is shown on page 122 with a half column subtracted from each side and a half row subtracted from both the top and bottom. Notice the different visual impact of this solution, which maintains the symmetry of the design.

#1 Elongated Dogtooth Border

#16 Odd Fellows   #5 Sunburst

#9 Kansas Troubles   #15 Rising Sun

#7 Dogtooth and Square Border

#5 Sunbeams Border

#13 Joseph's Coat   #1 Mariner's Compass

#3 Star and Cross   #10 Marigold

#9 Sawtooth Border

#12 Dogtooth Border

#14 Shaded Crossroad©

#6 Chips and Whetstones

#12 Wyoming Valley

#11 Sunflower

#15 Birds in Flight Border

DESIGN 1A: Asymmetrical arrangement created by using even numbers of blocks for each column and row.

DESIGN 1B: Symmetrical arrangement based on half columns and rows added to all four sides.

#1 Elongated Dogtooth Border

#1 Mariner's Compass   #1 Palm Leaf

APPENDIX A

CIRCULAR GRIDS

Draft circular blocks in any size you choose, following the instructions in the drafting exercise on page 12. The Multiples of Four grid should be used for designs requiring 8, 16, or 32 divisions. Use the Multiples of Five grid for designs requiring 10, 20, or 40 divisions. To make a block with 12, 24, or 48 divisions, use the Multiples of Six grid.

MULTIPLES OF FOUR GRID

Use for designs requiring 8, 16, or 32 divisions

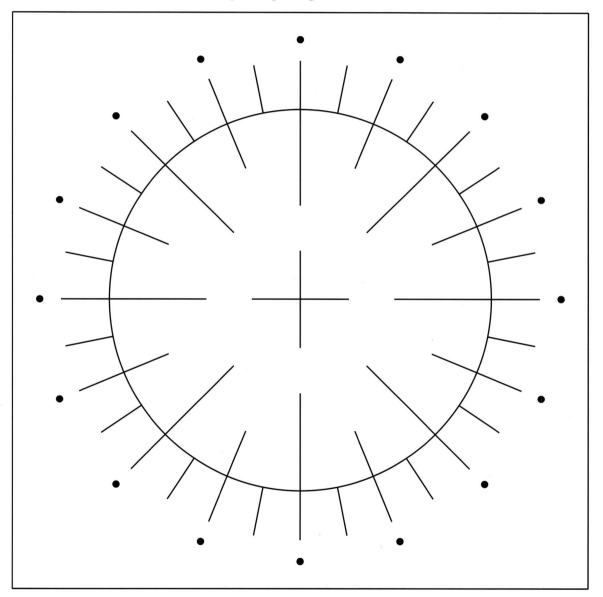

MULTIPLES OF FIVE GRID

Use for designs requiring 10, 20, or 40 divisions

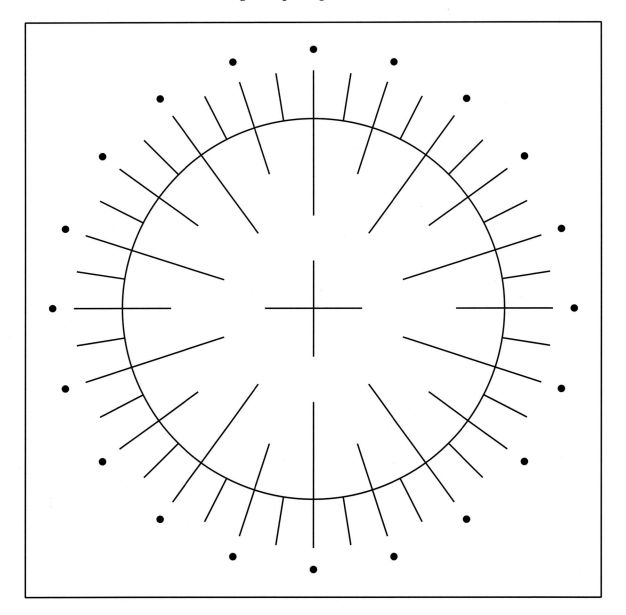

MULTIPLES OF SIX GRID

Use for designs requiring 12, 24, or 48 divisions

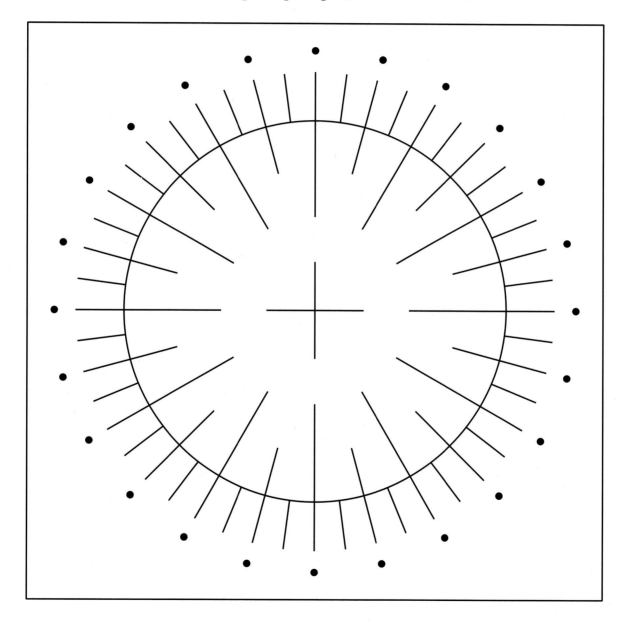

APPENDIX B

QUILT LAYOUTS TO COLOR

Line drawings of 35 blocks with borders are provided. Photocopy the drawings and use them to play with color strategies. When you have selected a color scheme, use the colored drawing as a guide for assembling the quilt.

DESIGN 1 – MARINER'S COMPASS & PALM LEAF

Navigating Compass Designs – Barbara Ann Caron

Design 2 – Mariner's Compass & Baltimore Belle

Design 3 – Mariner's Compass & Star and Cross

Design 4 – Slashed Star & Best of All

DESIGN 5 – SUNBURST & BLACKFORD'S BEAUTY

DESIGN 6 – CHIPS AND WHETSTONES & AMISH STAR

DESIGN 7 – ARABIAN STAR & WOOD LILY

Design 8 – Kansas Sunflower & Old Maid's Ramble

DESIGN 9 – SUNFLOWER & KANSAS TROUBLES

Design 10 – Marigold & Auntie's Favorite©

DESIGN 11 – SUNFLOWER & COUNTRY ROADS

Design 12 – Single Sunflower & Wyoming Valley

Design 13 – Wheel of Fortune & Joseph's Coat

DESIGN 14 – FEATHERED STAR & SHADED CROSSROAD©

Design 15 – Rising Sun & Wild Goose Chase

Design 16 – Sunbirds & Odd Fellows

APPENDIX C

SIX-INCH BLOCKS

Six-inch circular and setting blocks are provided to make small or miniature quilts. The templates are keyed to the information included with the 12-inch blocks in Chapter 4. One-half of each block pattern is provided.

DESIGN 1: PALM LEAF

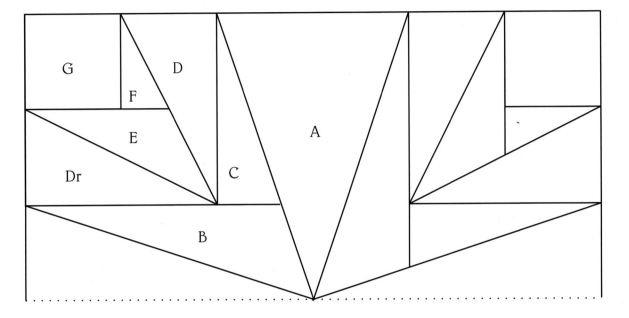

DESIGN 1: MARINER'S COMPASS

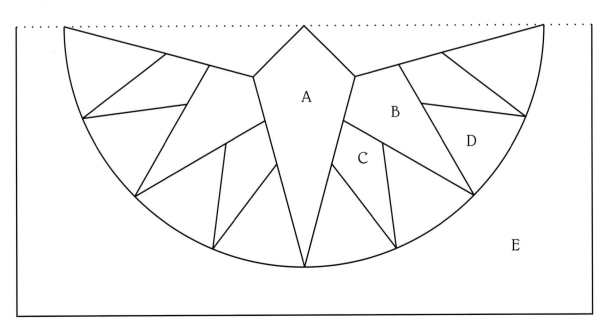

NAVIGATING COMPASS DESIGNS – BARBARA ANN CARON

DESIGN 2: BALTIMORE BELLE

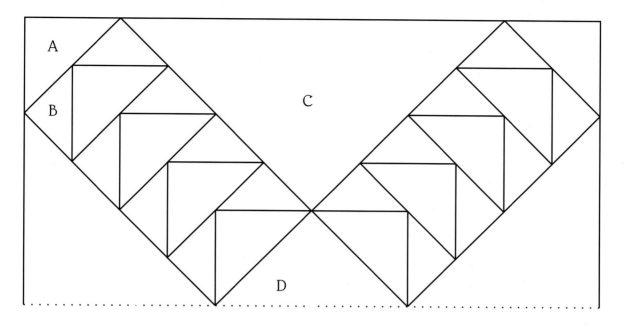

DESIGN 2: MARINER'S COMPASS

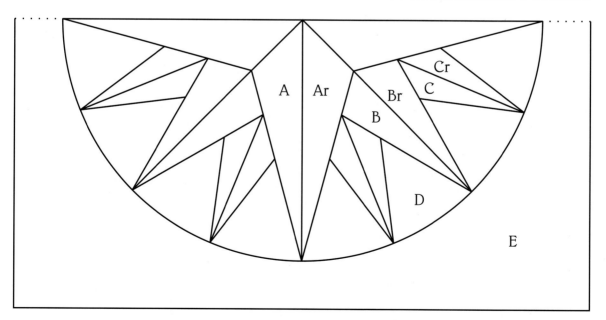

DESIGN 3: STAR AND CROSS

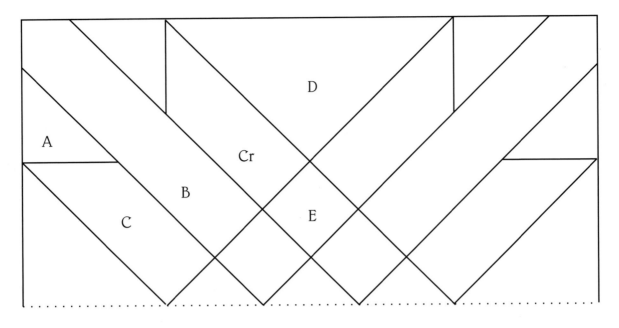

DESIGN 3: MARINER'S COMPASS

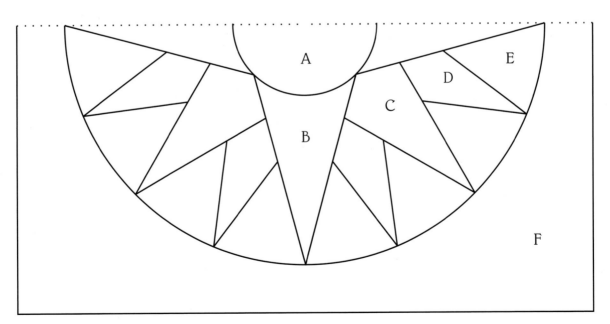

DESIGN 4: BEST OF ALL

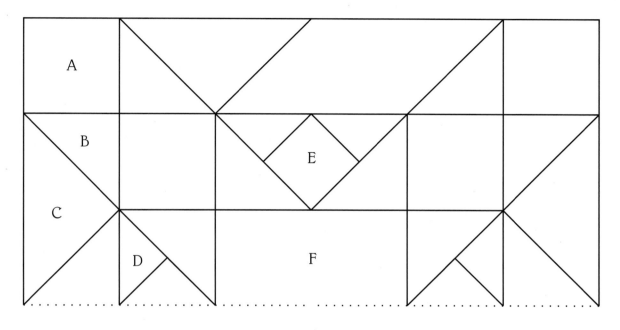

DESIGN 4: SLASHED STAR

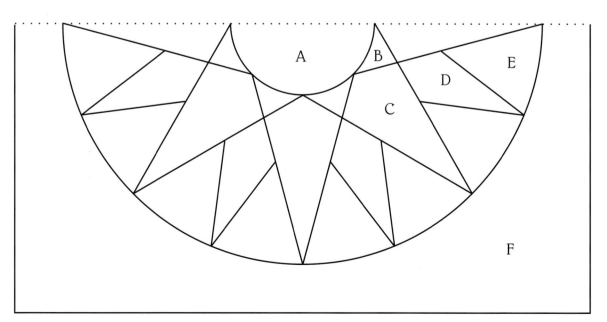

DESIGN 5: BLACKFORD'S BEAUTY

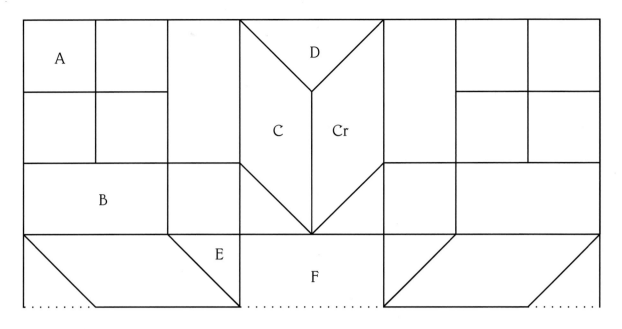

DESIGN 5: SUNBURST

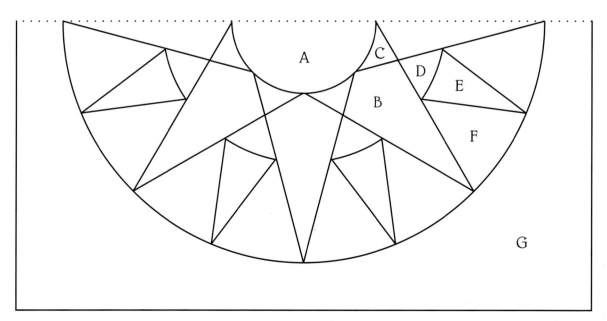

DESIGN 6: AMISH STAR

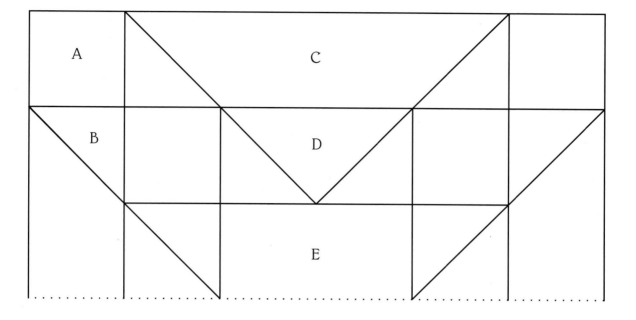

DESIGN 6: CHIPS AND WHETSTONES

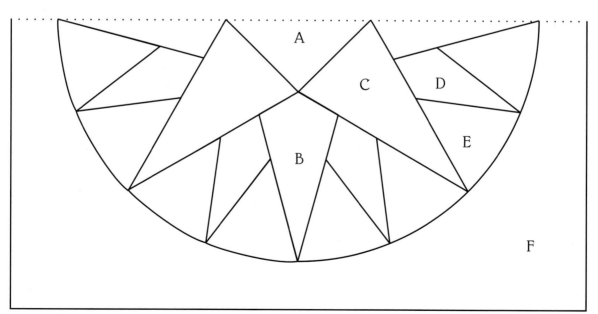

DESIGN 7: WOOD LILY

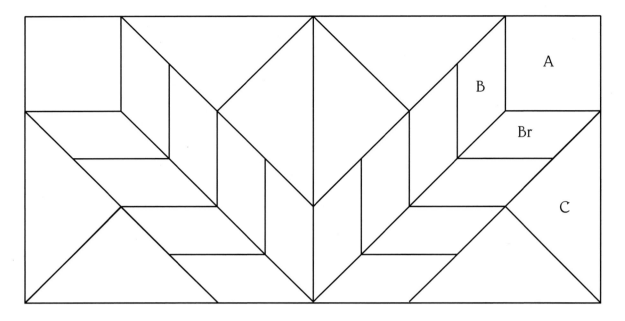

DESIGN 7: ARABIAN STAR

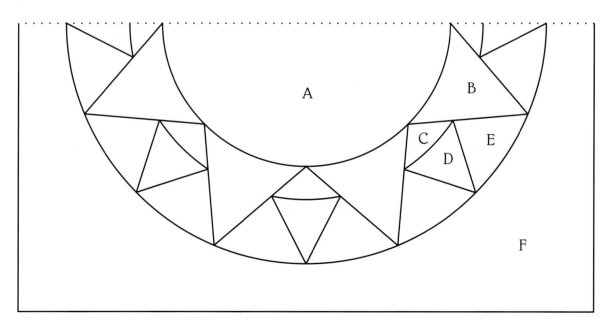

Design 8: Old Maid's Ramble

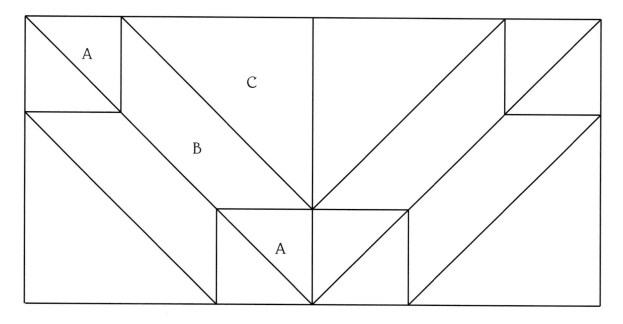

Design 8: Kansas Sunflower

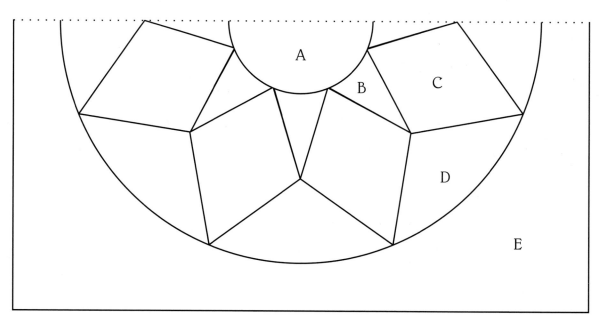

DESIGN 9: KANSAS TROUBLES

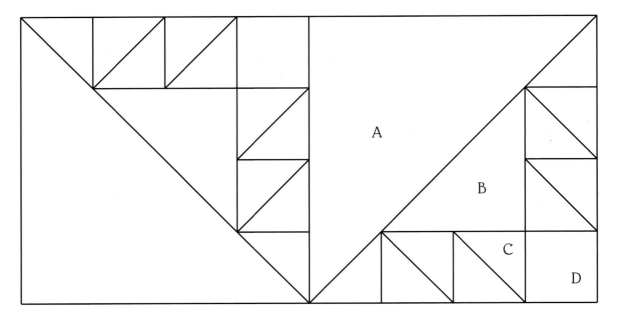

DESIGN 9: SUNFLOWER

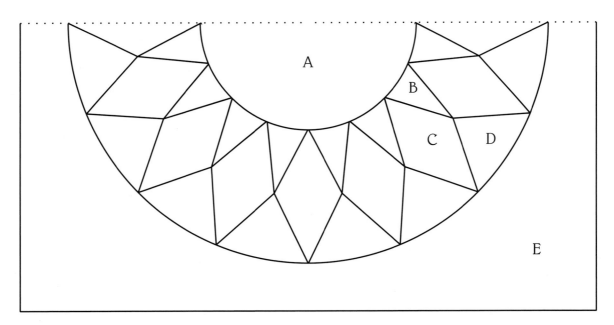

Design 10: Auntie's Favorite©

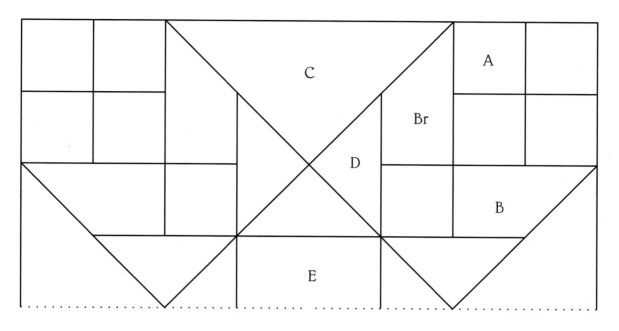

Design 10: Marigold

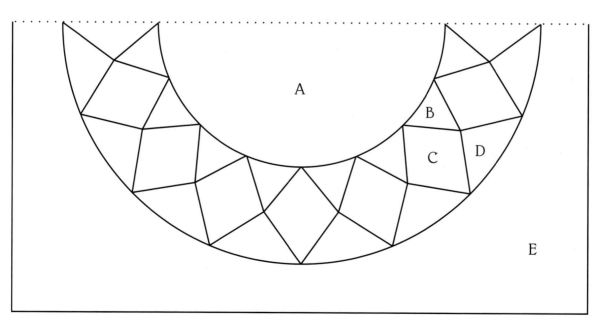

DESIGN 11: COUNTRY ROADS

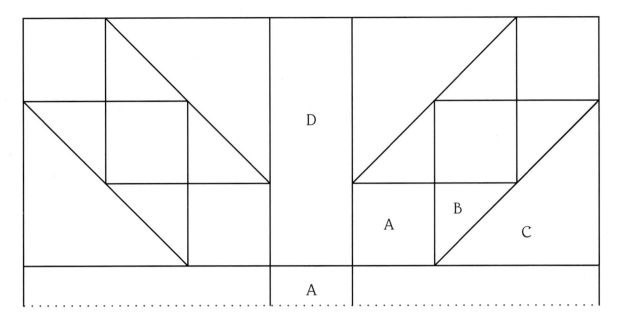

DESIGN 11: SUNFLOWER

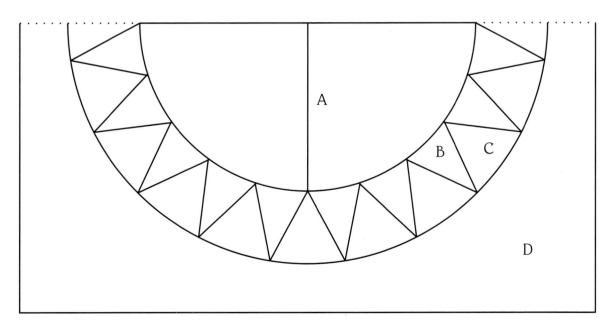

DESIGN 12: WYOMING VALLEY

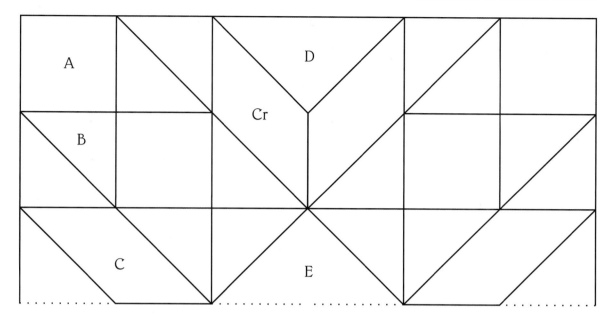

DESIGN 12: SINGLE SUNFLOWER

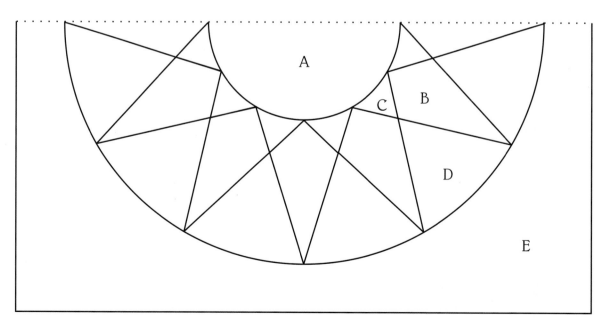

DESIGN 13: JOSEPH'S COAT

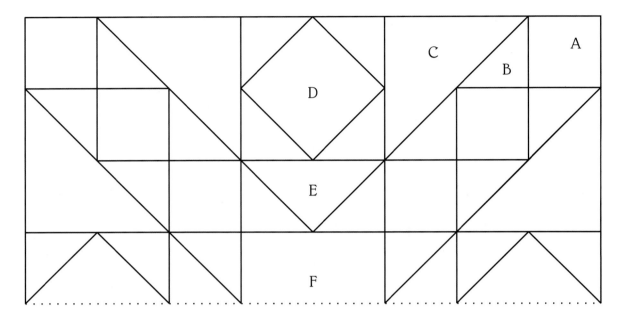

DESIGN 13: WHEEL OF FORTUNE

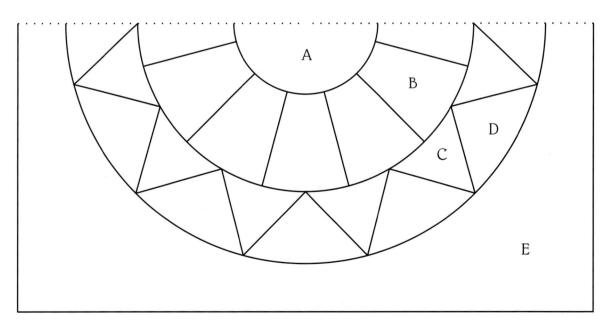

Design 14: Shaded Crossroad©

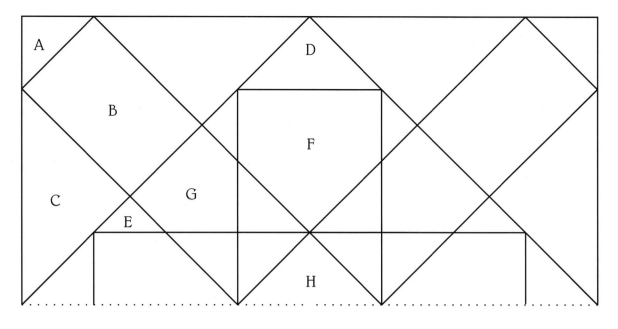

Design 14: Feathered Star

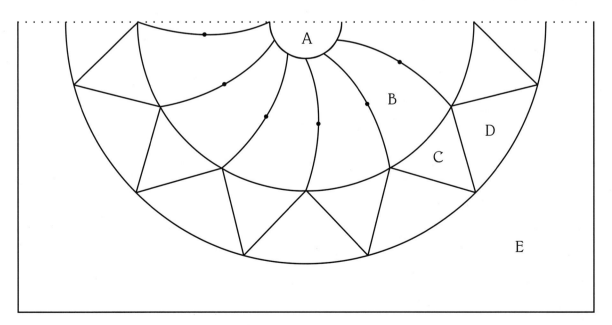

Design 15: Wild Goose Chase

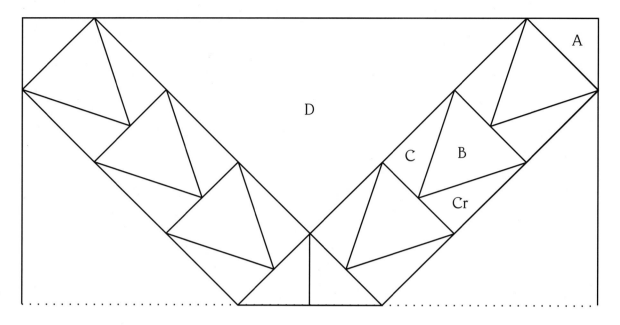

Design 15: Rising Sun

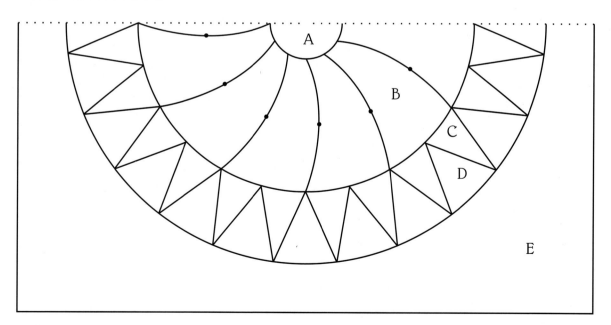

Design 16: Odd Fellows

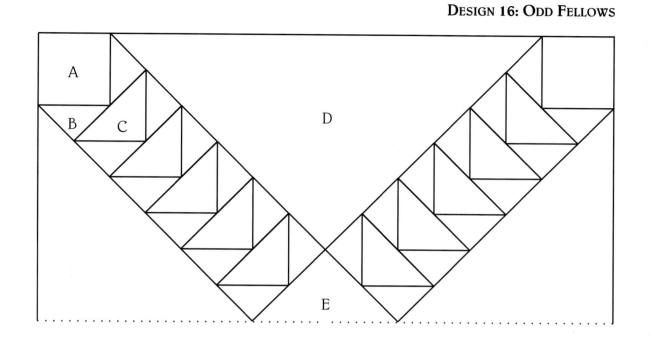

Design 16: Sunbirds

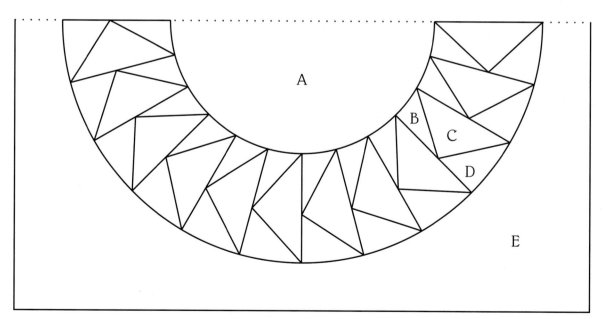

BIBLIOGRAPHY

BLOCKS

Brackman, Barbara, comp. *Encyclopedia of Pieced Quilt Patterns*. Paducah, KY: American Quilter's Society, 1993.

Beyer, Jinny. *Patchwork Portfolio*. McLean, VA: EPM Publications, Inc., 1989.

————. *The Quilter's Album of Blocks & Borders*. McLean, VA: EPM Publications, Inc., 1980.

Finley, Ruth. *Old Patchwork Quilts and the Women Who Made Them*. Philadelphia, PA: Lippincott, 1929.

Hall, Carrie A. and Rose G. Kretsinger. *The Romance of the Patchwork Quilt in America*. New York, NY: Dover Publications, Inc., 1988 (reprint of 1935 edition).

Hornung, Clarence P. *Handbook of Designs and Devices: 1836 Basic Designs and Their Variations*: New York, NY: Dover Publications, Inc., 1946 (reprint of 1932 edition).

Ickis, Marguerite. *The Standard Book of Quilt Making and Collecting*. New York, NY: Dover Publications, Inc., 1959 (reprint of 1949 edition).

Johnson, Mary Elizabeth. *A Garden of Quilts*. Birmingham, AL: Oxmoor House Inc., 1984.

Khin, Yvonne M. *The Collector's Dictionary of Quilt Names & Patterns*. Washington, DC: Acropolis Books, 1980.

Malone, Maggie. *500 Full-Size Patchwork Patterns*. New York, NY: Sterling Publishing Co., Inc., 1985.

————. *1001 Patchwork Designs*. New York, NY: Sterling Publishing Co., Inc., 1982.

Martin, Judy. *The Block Book*. Grinnell, IA: Crosley-Griffith Publishing Co., Inc., 1998.

Mathieson, Judy. *Mariner's Compass: An American Quilt Classic*. Lafayette, CA: C & T Publishing, 1987.

————. *Mariner's Compass Quilts: New Directions*. Lafayette, CA: C & T Publishing, 1995.

McKim, Ruby. *101 Patchwork Patterns*. New York, NY: Dover Publications, Inc., 1962 (reprint of 1931 edition).

Mills, Susan Winter. *Illustrated Index to Traditional American Quilt Patterns*. New York, NY: Arco Publishing, Inc., 1981.

Museum Quilts. New York, NY: Graphic Enterprises, nd.

Obenchain, Mabel, ed. *Keepsake Quilts*. New York, NY: Famous Features, nd.

Ouchi, Hajime. *Japanese Optical and Geometrical Art*. New York, NY: Dover Publications, Inc., 1977 (reprint of 1973 edition).

Weiss, Rita. *The Patchworker's Sewing Machine Quilt*. Northbrook, IL: American School of Needlework, 1982.

BORDERS

Browning, Bonnie K. *Borders & Finishing Touches*. Paducah, KY: American Quilter's Society, 1997.

Martin, Judy and Marsha McCloskey. *Pieced Borders: The Complete Resource*. Grinnell, IA: Crosley-Griffith, 1994.

Nyhan, Elizabeth F. *Treasury of Patchwork Borders: Full-Size Patterns for 76 Designs*. New York, NY: Dover, 1991.

Peters, Paulette. *Borders by Design: Creative Ways to Border Your Quilts*. Bothell, WA: That Patchwork Place, 1994.

COLOR AND FABRIC SELECTION

Beyer, Jinny. *Color Confidence for Quilters*. Gualala, CA: Quilt Digest Press, 1992.

Horton, Roberta. *Calico and Beyond: The Use of Patterned Fabric in Quilts*. Lafayette, CA: C & T Publishing, 1986.

McKelvey, Susan. *Color for Quilters II*. Millersville, MD: Wildflower Designs, 1993.

Penders, Mary Coyne. *Color and Cloth: The Quiltmaker's Ultimate Workbook*. San Francisco, CA: Quilt Digest Press, 1989.

Williamson, Darra Duffy. *Sensational Scrap Quilts*. Paducah, KY: American Quilter's Society, 1992.

Wolfrom, Joen. *The Magical Effects of Color*. Lafayette, CA: C & T Publishing, 1992.

DRAFTING

Beyer, Jinny. *Patchwork Patterns*. McLean, VA: EPM Publications, Inc., 1979.

FOUNDATION AND OTHER PIECING METHODS

Hall, Jane and Dixie Haywood. *Firm Foundations: Techniques and Quilt Blocks for Precision Piecing*. Paducah, KY: American Quilter's Society, 1996.

Doak, Carol. *Easy Machine Paper Piecing: 65 Quilt Blocks for Foundation Piecing*. Bothell, WA: That Patchwork Place, 1994.

————. *Easy Mix & Match Machine Paper Piecing*. Bothell, WA: That Patchwork Place, 1995.

Greenberg, Lesly-Claire. *Sewing on the Line: Fast & Easy Foundation Piecing*. Bothell, WA: That Patchwork Place, 1993.

Johannah, Barbara. *Half Square Triangles: Exploring Design*. Navarro, CA: Private Printing, 1987.

Rosintoski, Ellen. *Marvelous Mini Quilts for Foundation Piecing*. San Marcos, CA: American School of Needlework, 1994.

Rozmyn, Mia. *Freedom in Design: New Directions in Foundation Paper Piecing.* Bothell, WA: That Patchwork Place, 1995.

Wagner, Debra. *Striplate Piecing: Piecing Circle Designs with Speed and Accuracy.* Paducah, KY: American Quilter's Society, 1994.

MINIATURES

Gavatt, Tina M. *Heirloom Miniatures.* Paducah, KY: American Quilter's Society, 1990.

———. *Miniature Quilts: Connecting New & Old Worlds.* Paducah, KY: American Quilter's Society, 1996.

———. *Old Favorites in Miniature: Patterns & Instructions for Making Nineteen Miniature Quilts.* Paducah, KY: American Quilter's Society, 1993.

Johnson-Srebro, Nancy. *Miniature to Masterpiece: Perfect Piecing Secrets from a Prizewinning Quiltmaker.* Columbia Crossroads, PA: RCW, 1990.

Schafer, Becky. *Working in Miniature: A Machine Piecing Approach to Miniature Quilts.* Lafayette, CA: C & T Publishing, 1987.

QUILTING

Fons, Marianne. *Fine Feathers: A Quilter's Guide to Customizing Traditional Feather Quilting Designs.* Lafayette, CA: C & T Publishing, 1988.

Kimball, Jeana. *Loving Stitches: A Guide to Fine Hand Quilting.* Bothell, WA: That Patchwork Place, 1992.

Leone, Diana. *Fine Hand Quilting.* Los Alton, CA: Leone Publications, 1986.

Miller, Phyllis D. *Encyclopedia of Designs for Quilting.* Paducah, KY: American Quilter's Society, 1996.

Morris, Patricia J. *The Ins & Outs: Perfecting the Quilting Stitch.* Paducah, KY: American Quilter's Society, 1990.

Noble, Maurine. *Machine Quilting Made Easy!* Bothell, WA: That Patchwork Place, 1994

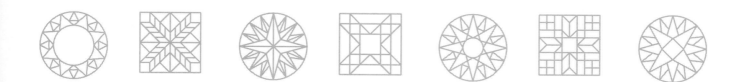

ABOUT THE AUTHOR

Barbara Ann Caron began making quilts in 1976. She teaches and lectures at local, regional, and national quilting seminars. Her interest in quilt design compelled her to acquire graduate degrees, a master's in design foundations and a doctorate in design history. She taught at the University of Northern Iowa and the University of Minnesota before joining the exhibits staff at the Minnesota Historical Society in 1997. Barbara is the author of *Tessellations & Variations*, published by AQS in 1995.

AQS BOOKS ON QUILTS

This is only a partial listing of the books on quilts that are available from the American Quilter's Society. AQS books are known the world over for their timely topics, clear writing, beautiful color photographs, and accurate illustrations and patterns. The following books are available from your local bookseller, quilt shop, or public library. If you are unable to locate certain titles in your area, you may order by mail from the AMERICAN QUILTER'S SOCIETY, P.O. Box 3290, Paducah, KY 42002-3290. Add $2.00 for postage for the first book ordered and 40¢ for each additional book. Include item number, title, and price when ordering. Allow 14 to 21 days for delivery. Customers with Visa, MasterCard, or Discover may phone in orders from 7:00 – 5:00 CST, Monday – Friday, Toll Free 1-800-626-5420.

4595	**Above & Beyond Basics**, Karen Kay Buckley	$18.95
2282	**Adapting Architectural Details for Quilts**, Carol Wagner	$12.95
4813	**Addresses & Birthdays**, compiled by Klaudeen Hansen **(HB)**	$14.95
4543	**American Quilt Blocks: 50 Patterns for 50 States**, Beth Summers	$16.95
4696	**Amish Kinder Komforts**, Bettina Havig	$14.95
4829	**Anita Shackelford: Surface Textures**, Anita Shackelford **(HB)**	$24.95
4899	**Appliqué Paper Greetings**, Elly Sienkiewicz **(HB)**	$24.95
3790	**Appliqué Patterns from Native American Beadwork Designs**, Dr. Joyce Mori	$14.95
2099	**Ask Helen: More About Quilting Designs**, Helen Squire	$14.95
2207	**Award-Winning Quilts: 1985-1987**	$24.95
2354	**Award-Winning Quilts: 1988-1989**	$24.95
3425	**Award-Winning Quilts: 1990-1991**	$24.95
3791	**Award-Winning Quilts: 1992-1993**	$24.95
4830	**Baskets: Celtic Style**, Scarlett Rose	$19.95
4832	**A Batch of Patchwork**, May T. Miller & Susan B. Burton	$18.95
4593	**Blossoms by the Sea: Making Ribbon Flowers for Quilts**, Faye Labanaris	$24.95
4898	**Borders & Finishing Touches**, Bonnie K. Browning	$16.95
4697	**Caryl Bryer Fallert: A Spectrum of Quilts, 1983-1995**, Caryl Bryer Fallert	$24.95
4626	**Celtic Geometric Quilts**, Camille Remme	$16.95
3926	**Celtic Style Floral Appliqué**, Scarlett Rose	$14.95
2208	**Classic Basket Quilts**, Elizabeth Porter & Marianne Fons	$16.95
2355	**Creative Machine Art**, Sharee Dawn Roberts	$24.95
4818	**Dear Helen, Can You Tell Me?** Helen Squire	$15.95
3399	**Dye Painting!** Ann Johnston	$19.95
4814	**Encyclopedia of Designs for Quilting**, Phyllis D. Miller **(HB)**	$34.95
3468	**Encyclopedia of Pieced Quilt Patterns**, compiled by Barbara Brackman	$34.95
3846	**Fabric Postcards**, Judi Warren	$22.95
4594	**Firm Foundations**, Jane Hall & Dixie Haywood	$18.95
4900	**Four Blocks Continued…**, Linda Giesler Carlson	$16.95
2381	**From Basics to Binding**, Karen Kay Buckley	$16.95
4526	**Gatherings: America's Quilt Heritage**, Kathlyn F. Sullivan	$34.95
2097	**Heirloom Miniatures**, Tina M. Gravatt	$9.95
4628	**Helen's Guide to quilting in the 21st century**, Helen Squire	$16.95
1906	**Irish Chain Quilts: A Workbook of Irish Chains**, Joyce B. Peaden	$14.95
3784	**Jacobean Appliqué: Book I, "Exotica,"** Campbell & Ayars	$18.95
4544	**Jacobean Appliqué: Book II, "Romantica,"** Campbell & Ayars	$18.95
3904	**The Judge's Task**, Patricia J. Morris	$19.95
4751	**Liberated Quiltmaking**, Gwen Marston **(HB)**	$24.95
4897	**Lois Smith's Machine Quiltmaking**, Lois Smith	$19.95
4523	**Log Cabin Quilts: New Quilts from an Old Favorite**	$14.95
4545	**Log Cabin with a Twist**, Barbara T. Kaempfer	$18.95
4815	*Love to Quilt:* **Bears, Bears, Bears**, Karen Kay Buckley	$14.95
4833	*Love to Quilt:* **Broderie Perse: The Elegant Quilt**, Barbara W. Barber	$14.95
4890	*Love to Quilt:* **Dye & Discharge**, Sara Newberg King	$14.95
4598	*Love to Quilt:* **Men's Vests**, Alexandra Capadalis Dupré	$14.95
4816	*Love to Quilt:* **Necktie Sampler Blocks**, Janet B. Elwin	$14.95
4753	*Love to Quilt:* **Penny Squares**, Willa Baranowski	$12.95
4995	**Magic Stack-n-Whack Quilts**, Bethany S. Reynolds	$19.95
4911	**Mariner's Compass Quilts: New Quilts from an Old Favorite**	$16.95
4752	**Miniature Quilts: Connecting New & Old Worlds**, Tina M. Gravatt	$14.95
4514	**Mola Techniques for Today's Quilters**, Charlotte Patera	$18.95
3330	**More Projects and Patterns**, Judy Florence	$18.95
1981	**Nancy Crow: Quilts and Influences**, Nancy Crow	$29.95
3331	**Nancy Crow: Work in Transition**, Nancy Crow	$12.95
4828	**Nature, Design & Silk Ribbons**, Cathy Grafton	$18.95
3332	**New Jersey Quilts**, The Heritage Quilt Project of New Jersey	$29.95
3927	**New Patterns from Old Architecture**, Carol Wagner	$12.95
2153	**No Dragons on My Quilt**, Jean Ray Laury	$12.95
4627	**Ohio Star Quilts: New Quilts from an Old Favorite**	$16.95
3469	**Old Favorites in Miniature**, Tina Gravatt	$15.95
4831	**Optical Illusions for Quilters**, Karen Combs	$22.95
4515	**Paint and Patches: Painting on Fabrics with Pigment**, Vicki L. Johnson	$18.95
5098	**Pineapple Quilts, New Quilts from an Old Favorite**	$16.95
4513	**Plaited Patchwork**, Shari Cole	$19.95
3928	**Precision Patchwork for Scrap Quilts**, Jeannette Tousley Muir	$12.95
4779	**Protecting Your Quilts: A Guide for Quilt Owners, Second Edition**	$6.95
4542	**A Quilted Christmas**, edited by Bonnie Browning	$18.95
2380	**Quilter's Registry**, Lynne Fritz	$9.95
3467	**Quilting Patterns from Native American Designs**, Dr. Joyce Mori	$12.95
3470	**Quilting with Style**, Gwen Marston & Joe Cunningham	$24.95
2284	**Quiltmaker's Guide: Basics & Beyond**, Carol Doak	$19.95
4918	**Quilts by Paul D. Pilgrim: Blending the Old & the New**, Gerald E. Roy	$16.95
2257	*Quilts:* **The Permanent Collection – MAQS**	$9.95
3793	*Quilts:* **The Permanent Collection – MAQS Volume II**	$9.95
3789	**Roots, Feathers & Blooms**, Linda Giesler Carlson	$16.95
4512	**Sampler Quilt Blocks from Native American Designs**, Dr. Joyce Mori	$14.95
3796	**Seasons of the Heart & Home: Quilts for a Winter's Day**, Jan Patek	$18.95
3761	**Seasons of the Heart & Home: Quilts for Summer Days**, Jan Patek	$18.95
2357	**Sensational Scrap Quilts**, Darra Duffy Williamson	$24.95
4783	**Silk Ribbons by Machine**, Jeanie Sexton	$15.95
3929	**The Stori Book of Embellishing**, Mary Stori	$16.95
3903	**Straight Stitch Machine Appliqué**, Letty Martin	$16.95
3792	**Striplate Piecing**, Debra Wagner	$24.95
5012	**Take-Away Appliqué**, Suzanne Marshall	$22.95
3930	**Tessellations & Variations**, Barbara Ann Caron	$14.95
3788	**Three-Dimensional Appliqué**, Anita Shackelford	$24.95
4596	**Ties, Ties, Ties: Traditional Quilts from Neckties**, Janet B. Elwin	$19.95
3931	**Time-Span Quilts: New Quilts from Old Tops**, Becky Herdle	$16.95
4919	**Transforming Fabric**, Carolyn Dahl	$29.95
2029	**A Treasury of Quilting Designs**, Linda Goodmon Emery	$14.95
3847	**Tricks with Chintz**, Nancy S. Breland	$14.95
5014	**The Wholecloth Garment Stori**, Mary Stori	$19.95
2286	**Wonderful Wearables: A Celebration of Creative Clothing**, Virginia Avery	$24.95
4812	**Who's Who in American Quilting**, edited by Bonnie Browning **(HB)**	$49.95
4956	**Variegreat! New Dimensions in Traditional Quilts**, Linda Glantz	$19.95
4972	**20th Century Quilts**, Cuesta Benberry and Joyce Gross	$ 9.95